FINDING

Your

NORTH

FINDING

Your

NORTH

Self-Help Strategies
for Science-Related Careers

Frederick L. Moore, Ph.D.
& Michael L. Penn Jr., M.D., Ph.D.

PotentSci LLC
Emeryville, California 94608

Published by PotentSci LLC
1249 66th Street
Emeryville, CA 94608
www.findingyournorth.com

Publisher's Cataloging-in-Publication Data

Finding your north : self-help strategies for science-related careers / edited by Frederick L. Moore and Michael L. Penn Jr. – Emeryville, CA : PotentSci, LLC, 2005.

p. ; cm.

ISBN: 0-9766205-0-2

ISBN13: 978-0-9766205-0-1

1. Science—Vocational guidance. 2. Educational counseling. I. Title. II. Moore, Frederick L. III. Penn Jr., Michael L.

Q147 .F56 2005

500.023—dc22   2005921676

Book production and coordination by Jenkins Group, Inc. • www.bookpublishing.com
Interior design by Chad Miller
Cover design by Chris Rhoads

Printed in the United States of America
09 08 07 06 05 • 5 4 3 2 1

DEDICATION

This book is written in loving memory of Dr. Margaret Lucille Penn. We also would like to thank our friends and family who made this dream possible. In particular, the editors would like to acknowledge Anthony D. Williams for his steadfast support from the very beginning of this project. And to all of the youth of this generation and beyond, always remember to look onward and upward towards the light!

CONTENTS

You Can Do It

By Herbert Boyer, Ph.D.

A s a senior in high school fifty years ago in Derry, Pennsylvania, I would have loved to have been able to read a copy of this book. Compared with today's standards, the counseling that was provided for my future was quite limited. A person's skills, indicative of a potential profession, were evaluated by a hand-eye coordination test. After I had taken this test and was anxiously awaiting the results, I thought that I would surely be singled out to be an airplane pilot or a brain surgeon. Interestingly, when the results were announced, I was summarily told that I would be well suited to become an auto mechanic. The idea of becoming an auto mechanic was perplexing to me, since my family owned no car and I had no idea how to even change an oil filter. We were also given two IQ tests. I was devastated to find out that my IQ was only average. In any case, I knew that I would not be a very talented auto mechanic, so I opted to attend a nearby college. I somehow managed to muddle my way through college and graduate school, and I have no regrets about the outcome of my science education and careers; however, this book would have provided me with very helpful insights into the academic process. It would have challenged me to maintain balance while I navigated this path and, equally important, it would have provided me with comfort in knowing that the trials, tribulations, and self-doubt that I experienced during my education and career were not confined to me alone.

Since students in today's society have access to high school counselors, college counselors, psychologists, professional college and graduate school test-taking courses, and numerous self-help books. Why might they need yet another self-help book about preparing for a career in medicine or the life sciences? The value of this book is closely entwined with the very personal and often moving accounts of the authors' own educational and career experiences. Interestingly, minorities, who make up only a small fraction of people obtaining science degrees, write all of the chapters in this book. This fact allows this book to uniquely motivate and prepare minorities for science-related careers. However, the lessons, experiences, and strategies contained in this book are extremely valuable to any student who is interested in pursuing a science-related career. The authors who write these chapters are outstanding role models for anyone.

In the first section of the book, chapter 1, the authors confront the reader's motivation for wanting to be a scientist or physician by challenging the readers to think about their personality, strengths and weaknesses, and the type of experiences they want from life. They clearly caution readers that both careers require an interest that borders on compulsiveness and a dedication of time that can be oppressive. Yet, in parallel, the authors begin to lay the groundwork for the limitless possibilities available with a science and medical background. Taken as a whole, it becomes more important as people embarks on these types of careers that they develop ways to keep balance in their lives. Fortunately, the author of the second chapter provides a personal account of how to balance your life while pursuing such a demanding career. In chapter 3, the author shares some insightful approaches to understanding how you naturally think and provides strategies to maximize your learning experience. The outline of this chapter resonated with my learning experience. In particular, I, too, found that explaining a subject was the best way for me to understand the material. One of my learning deficiencies while in school was a hesitation to ask questions, because I feared that people might think I was ignorant. During my time as a professor at UC San Francisco, I told my students that there were no dumb questions, but there are dumb answers. The author of this chapter provided good arguments for why the readers should question what they read and learn in school. In addition, I agree with the author's notion that there are many benefits to working in study groups. I believe that interacting with your peers in group discussion is extremely valuable, and developing this skill will be increasingly important as you enter the professional realm. You will find that understanding how your colleagues think, and responding to them accordingly, will be essential. Even Einstein relied on his colleagues for help!

In chapter 4, the author shares his unique perspective on how to apply to graduate/professional schools. I understand that admission to any graduate/professional school requires a good deal of preparation, and the material covered in this chapter adequately covers all of those bases. I served on the admission committees for both graduate and medical schools for quite a number of years, and I understand the weight that is placed on interviews. They most often determine if one is admitted to a graduate/professional school. My advice during the interview process is to keep this maxim in mind: "Be true to yourself." I remember vividly my first medical student applicant. She was a thirty-year-old IBM executive who decided to become a physician. She had returned to UC Berkeley to obtain her required science courses, and at the same time, she worked to support herself and her ailing mother. Because of her sincerity, as well as her academic and professional credentials, I championed her admission to medical school, despite the bias at the time against admitting mature students and female students. I was elated when she graduated from medical school at UC San Francisco and was presented with the Gold-Headed Cane Award, a prestigious honor bestowed by her classmates.

The second section of the book is devoted to graduate school in the life sciences and medical school. When I read chapter 5, it revived within me many memories of my graduate school days. I could easily relate to the author when she talked about the anxiety of whether or not a thesis would ever materialize. I believe this chapter is a must-read for students who want to pursue an advanced degree in the life sciences, and I endorse the suggested guidelines. Chapter 6 is a moving personal account of the trials of the graduate school experience. After reading this chapter, you will realize that your personal trying experiences are no excuse for not succeeding. The next chapter in section two describes the emotions and factors that are encountered when one has to make a difficult life decision that confronts many students, a career choice change. In reading this chapter, I was reminded of a similar incident from my undergraduate days. An acquaintance of mine was a seminarian who, after several arduous years in the seminary and some major introspection, decided to leave the priesthood. He went on to become a prominent judge in western Pennsylvania. Again, remember the maxim "be true to yourself" and you will be guided. Any intelligent person can change his or her mind.

In the second half of section two of the book, the authors describe the culture of medicine. If you are interested in being a practicing physician, I recommend reading chapter 8 several times. This chapter is an A-to-Z guide that is an engaging and detailed account of not only medical education, but the experiences of a real physician. After reading this chapter you will be able to make up your mind, without any equivocation, as to whether being a physician is your desire. In chapter 9, the author reiterates many observations of the previous chapter, but they are presented with a lighter and delightful emphasis. You are advised to not become a physician for the money, because this motivation will not sustain you during your medical journey. The author of this chapter provided a pragmatic list of tips for being successful during your undergraduate years and during medical school. Trust her... she's a doctor!

I found the last chapter in section two particularly moving and honest. The author describes his self-doubt and periods of depression during his medical experience. This chapter hit close to home with me because it painfully reminded me of similar feelings from my graduate school days. These experiences do not augur an unsuccessful career, but rather provide opportunities to more deeply explore your commitment and motivations. The take-home lesson is to use your experiences as a competitive edge.

The last section of the book is another must-read. The title is "Resisting Conformity: Charting Your Own Course." How I love this title. Chapter 11 describes how you can leverage your strengths and education to shape a productive and rewarding career. The author's career proves that success can be derived in part from personal characteristics obtained not through education, but rather through understanding and utilizing your innate talents as well as through life experiences and self-awareness. She shares how she was able to use traits like confidence and determination to navigate her career. In addition, this author also provides one of the most complete and descriptive lists of career opportunities in the biomedical sciences. This chapter will be an invaluable compendium for science-oriented students.

This impressive book concludes with a chapter written by the coeditors. The philosophical challenge of this chapter is to discover your true purpose. I must admit forthright that I did not do well in philosophy courses (I flunked metaphysics), but nonetheless, this chapter is very thought-provoking. In addition, this chapter stimulates and challenges the reader to do some soul searching, which is something that all human beings should do.

In closing, I must say that I have thoroughly enjoyed this book. I believe the experiences shared by the authors are invaluable tools that can be used to shape the next generation of physicians and scientists. I will conclude by sharing with you two tenets propounded by the Benedictines of my undergraduate days: One's education never ends, and education prepares you for the tribulations and joys of life. Good luck to you, reader—you are the future.

Beating the Odds: Preparing High-Achieving Minority Students for Careers in Science

By Freeman A. Hrabowski III, Ph.D.

The editors of this book, Drs. Frederick Moore and Michael Penn Jr., along with the book's contributors—all minorities—serve as excellent role models and provide inspiration for this volume's readers. All have earned science Ph.D.'s, M.D.'s, or M.D./Ph.D.'s, and most are currently working as scientific researchers or physicians at some of the nation's most prestigious universities or in the private sector. In their chapters, the authors provide extremely useful advice based on their own personal experiences, discussing proven strategies for academic success.

I identify with much of what the authors have to say, because I vividly recall the major transition I made thirty-five years ago upon graduating from historically black Hampton University and entering graduate school in mathematics at the University of Illinois at Urbana-Champaign. The Hampton experience, involving a predominantly black student population and an integrated faculty, allowed me to get to know well my professors from various racial and ethnic backgrounds in a setting that strongly encouraged personal interaction among students and faculty. Studying at Hampton not only prepared me well academically for graduate work, but also taught me that I needed to believe in myself, that my classmates and I had a special mission to become leaders in our chosen fields, and that even though I was different from others, those differences could be important strengths.

When I arrived in Urbana-Champaign, however, I discovered that it may be easier academically than socially to prepare for the experiences of being, in most cases, the only African-American or minority student in a classroom and of almost never seeing a professor who looks like you. My graduate work (first in mathematics and later in statistics and higher education administration) and my professional experiences since earning my doctorate three decades ago have taught me some important lessons that may be helpful to others whose backgrounds are similar to mine.

First, in any university setting, undergraduate and graduate students can find professors and staff members from various racial and ethnic backgrounds who are willing to be supportive. The challenge each student faces is to identify those individuals. One approach is to ask other students about faculty members' reputations. Another approach, especially for graduate students, involves simply talking to a variety of faculty about their research to determine your interest in their specialties and to observe how each faculty member interacts with students. Professors tend to interact more favorably when they see that students have a keen interest in their fields.

Based largely on my experiences at Hampton and the University of Illinois, my colleagues and I established the Meyerhoff Scholars Program at the University of Maryland, Baltimore County, designed to prepare minority undergraduates (and, more recently, graduate fellows) in science and engineering to succeed and to go on to successful graduate work and ultimately successful careers in science and engineering fields. The program has become one of the most successful of its kind in the country.[1] Those efforts have led to the development and refinement of several programmatic components that have proven to be helpful to students.

We also have identified several important personal skills and values that students should strive to develop. These attributes, which can help students strengthen their academic performance and career preparation, include (1) knowing both one's strengths and those areas in need of improvement; (2) identifying strategies for motivating oneself to continue working hard; (3) developing a "thick skin" and the willingness to welcome and learn from constructive criticism; (4) developing leadership skills by being involved in extracurricular activities and learning from the successful leadership practices of other students; and (5) engaging in community service to help others less fortunate and, equally important, to learn about oneself and develop one's character. This last point is especially important, because minority children and students desperately need young role models who can strengthen their support systems.

In summary, successful undergraduate and graduate students in science, engineering, and medicine—especially minority students—are those who (1) are passionate about their discipline, showing enthusiasm and a keen interest in their work; (2) understand the importance of hard work and truly believe they will work as hard as necessary to succeed; (3) interact with fellow students and with faculty and staff for purposes of collaboration; and (4), most important, believe in themselves and know, deep down, that they will succeed.

In the following chapters, Dr. Frederick Moore, Dr. Michael Penn Jr., and their fellow authors write passionately about their successful academic experiences that have prepared them for rewarding careers in science and medicine. Their passion is contagious, their advice is invaluable, and I commend them for their commitment to helping others—especially underrepresented minorities—to be successful too.

FOOTNOTES

[1] J. Mervis, *The BEST Programs in Academia*, Science 301 (August 22, 2003), 1030.

An Introduction from the Editors

This book is designed to be a guide that you can utilize to identify the source of your passion and tap into that source so you can use that energy to fuel your exploration of life. This book is about *"Finding Your North."* If you are interested in science, you may be wondering why we are utilizing a self-help approach here. We, the editors of this book, have been where you are. We've struggled with physics and organic chemistry. We've questioned whether or not we chose the right career path (and still do!). We've been intimidated by the sheer volume of information in science and medicine. We've wished for someone or something to help make our journey more clearly reflective of who we are as individuals. We wanted to find *our* North.

Our vision for this book grew out of our passion for empowering students. Together, we have over twenty years' experience mentoring and advising students—not to mention being mentored and advised ourselves during that same time period. We realized that there was a niche that needed to be filled. While the pursuit of higher education in science and medicine can be tremendously exciting and rewarding, it can also be a lonely and stressful journey. Consequently, those who embark on this road will no doubt find themselves in need of an adviser—someone who can help make sense of all the emotions and doubts that will arise along the way. However, students also need a resource that provides them with honest and practical advice about how to maintain a proper perspective when they are challenged during their academic pursuits. Choosing a career path is a serious exercise that should be approached with much care and thought. *Finding Your North* will give you that road map to follow your own unique path to personal and career fulfillment.

Finding Your North is a unique book. Unlike most other career advice books, the contributing authors in this book have all been in your shoes. They have struggled with the very questions you're wrestling with right now. They want to help guide you away from the mistakes they've made and lead you toward the key elements of their own successes. The approach that the collective authors have taken with this book is not a one-size-fits-all. Instead, you will read very personal accounts of their experiences— almost as if you were having an intimate conversation with each of them. You will hear stories of personal triumph and tragedy. You will read about fears and insecurities as well as faith and confidence. In this book, you will learn about the variety of experiences that students like you have had while pursuing their passions in science and medicine. The purpose of this book is not to ensure that all of our readers get into their top schools of choice for graduate or medical school. Rather, the purpose of this book is to empower you to make appropriate career choices for yourselves that will lead to happy and fulfilling science-related careers. We hope that this book will illuminate choices for you that will honor your strengths and talents, but respect your limitations and areas that still need development. There is only one appropriate path to take: yours, and no one else's. So as you read the personal experiences contained within these pages, place yourself into the authors' perspective. Pretend that you are living their experiences. You will truly take away from this book everything that you put into it.

Section One

Reading the Compass:
Make Sure You
Are Headed in
the Right Direction

CHAPTER 1
Is Science for Me?

By Tanya Henneman, Ph.D., Frederick L. Moore, Ph.D., and Chad Womack, Ph.D.

I s science for me? This can be a very difficult question to answer. In the past, people who had an affinity for science were placed into one of two categories: the intense scientists who knew from birth that they wanted to perform laboratory experiments and the practicing physicians who had a burning desire to heal people through the art of medicine. In the twenty-first century, the concepts of science and medicine are different. Acquiring scientific knowledge and learning to apply scientific principles can lead to a diverse array of educational and career paths. Yes, if you love science you could use your intellectual prowess to develop an effective vaccine for HIV/AIDS or use knowledge of the human genome to find ways to cure diseases by gene therapy. You could also utilize a background in science as an investment banker who seeks to exploit the perfect opportunity to invest in the biotech industry, or as someone who helps to guide and shape science policy at the highest levels of government. Then again, a science background could help you to further facilitate the art of healing through Western or ancient forms of medicine such as acupuncture, herbal therapies, or Ayurveda. The sky is the limit, and this book is charged with laying down a foundation that will help you to be successful in a science graduate or medical school program; but more importantly, this book is aimed at opening your mind to the infinite possibilities available in life and utilizing science as a means to achieve them.

Who Are Scientists?

When some people picture scientists, they think of Dr. Jekyll and Mr. Hyde. They typically imagine a nerdy white man wearing a white lab coat and a pocket protector. Scientists are thought to be devoid of creativity and imagination, with only the ability to think linearly and logically. However, this image is very misleading if you don't know what scientists do. For instance, the true nature of a scientist is to ask questions and to discover novel ways to answer them. At the heart of every scientist is the desire to understand the quality or aspect of something at the deepest level possible. One example of such a scientist was George Washington Carver, who had the curiosity and drive to explore and understand, at the deepest level possible, the utility of a single plant. In his lifetime, he discovered over 325 uses for the peanut. It is this mode of thinking that drives people to invent, discover, and excel, yet when it is coupled with other qualities, it can help a scientist to become even more successful. One of these qualities is creative intelligence.

Possessing "book smarts," or the ability to score high on an IQ test, isn't a complete indicator of intelligence. The ability to link the creative and imaginative parts of oneself with the rational and logical parts is a form of creative intelligence; moreover, when a synergy is created between learned knowledge and original ideas, it allows for new and unique insights. Albert Einstein said in a 1929 interview, "I am enough of an artist to draw freely upon my imagination. Imagination is more important than knowledge.

Knowledge is limited. Imagination encircles the world." Mastering knowledge from books, lectures, and articles is only one part of a greater set of skills that is needed to have a successful career in science. Scientists are able to amass and process large volumes of information in such a way that connections, relationships, and pathways are discovered in a unique way.

Persistence and patience are other qualities that are necessary to be a successful scientist. The time that it takes to complete a set of lab experiments is unpredictable. A scientist can spend weeks, months, and even years setting up and executing experiments, only to discover that the proposed hypothesis is untrue. Persistence is part of the driving force that allows a scientist to keep searching and trying to succeed; however, when it is coupled with patience, these qualities can make a powerful combination. There are many times, when scientists perform experiments that the answer or next steps are not obvious. When patience is lacking, many people perform the experiments again without *really* analyzing the root of the failed experiment. The scientists who tend to be successful more often than others are those who have the patience and calmness to take a step back from the experiment and methodically analyze the data, detach emotionally from the desired outcome, and figure out alternative approaches to solving the problem. This ability is important with any type of problem solving, but it becomes even more important with experiments, where the effort and preparation invested is enormous and you're also competing with time. The exciting thing about uncovering these qualities within yourself or developing them through pursuing an advanced science degree is that once you learn them, you can utilize this approach to problem solving in any aspect of life.

Am I Better Suited for Medicine?

Just as we articulated a few characteristics that people possess who tend to be successful researchers, people who tend to gravitate toward medicine have other characteristics. For instance, do you like to care for others? As a practicing physician you are responsible for the lives of your patients. The best physicians are naturally comfortable with this role and are energized and motivated by it. Although aspiring medical students have to develop a certain comfort level with their knowledge and skills, the compassion that they have toward the health of others and the commitment to be students in the art of healing are what drive many students through the rigors of medical school and residency.

But since we are on this topic, let's take a closer look at what it means to care for others. There are other factors that you must take into consideration when you answer this question. For example, can you emotionally deal with the loss of another life? If not, there may be a field within medicine (dermatology, ophthalmology, etc.) that is better suited for your personality. Also, some people have a hard time being around extremely sick patients, who may drain their energy. Are your emotions and judgments easily swayed by negative energy or sick people? The best physicians have developed the ability to detach from their patients in a safe way, yet can connect to them in a healthy and productive way. For example, one caveat is when a physician completely detaches emotionally from patients; he or she may lose the compassion that is necessary to heal those patients. Conversely, if one connects too strongly to patients, it could cause emotional and physical strain, which could affect the ability to treat them over the long term. There is a fine line that needs to be developed to maintain a healthy balance between the health of your patients and your own health.

Another important question that you should ask yourself, if you are considering a career in medicine is, "Am I culturally sensitive to others?" The best physicians tend to be culturally sensitive to their patients in ways that allow the patient to open up. For many ethnic groups in this country, going to the doctor is a challenging process, based on a lack of trust of the medical community or a physician's lack of understanding on the role culture plays with health and well-being. The manner in which a physician communicates with patients and understands their needs and concerns, which can be culturally sensitive, can make a difference in the amount or level of information that is revealed to the doctor. Health is such a personal issue that many people have a hard time admitting to and/or sharing their habits or behaviors with a doctor. As you think about a career in medicine, you should be conscious of your strengths and weaknesses and ask yourself, "Is this the best way for me to utilize my talents?"

Conclusion

The exciting thing about scratching the surface of qualities associated with people who have successful careers in research and medicine is that you may have some of these qualities or all of these qualities, and may decide that a foundation in science or medicine may be only a stepping-stone in your life's path. The following chapters in this book will further your understanding of medicine, science, and alternate careers in the sciences and empower you to make a more informed choice.

CHAPTER 2

Striving for Balance
while in School

By Kyra Bobinet, M.D.

I t's 9 a.m., and I show up on time for my Thursday small group, which is led by a prominent cardiologist. Many experiences filled the past twenty-four hours: volunteering in the afternoon, getting an evening call from my depressed mom, running a mouse experiment in the lab until 2 a.m., cuddling up to my sleeping spouse, waking up late, throwing on clothes and barely making the shuttle. I was still reviewing these events in my mind when I noticed that all of my fellow students had case files in their hands. To my horror, I realized that we had homework! Let's face it—everyone forgets things. But I've noticed that when I forget major responsibilities or commitments, it is a clear sign that I am out of balance.

Balance as a Dynamic Process

As I peer into the busy lives of people in today's society, it seems that many people's lives are out of balance. Not surprisingly, our higher degree programs are intentionally designed to immerse students in study. Oftentimes, this immersion is at the expense of our self-care and balance. Interestingly, every medical student I have ever talked to has mentioned that they want "balance." Yet what can we *really* expect in the pursuit of this mystical state we call "balance"? Does it really exist? And if so, is it attainable by students in higher degree programs?

Let's suppose that we stand still, close our eyes, and pay close attention to our body. We notice that to stay balanced for any length of time requires many ongoing adjustments from all parts of our musculature. Our bodies have many internal shifts and changes, and our thoughts, blood flow, breath, and food digestion can change our stable state from one moment to the next. This is one illustration of the true nature of balance as a dynamic process.

The concept of possessing a dynamic mental and physical state of existence isn't a new idea. For over a thousand years, Tibetan scholars have studied the correlation between thoughts and emotions. They understand that when one has strong emotions, there is an increase in the number and frequency of thoughts. Conversely, they have observed that increasing the number and speed of thoughts consistently generates emotions. This means that as our minds are intensely engaged in study, we might experience—as a by-product—an increase in emotionality. Yes, it seems our bodies have multiple dynamic processes to maintain balance, and it may seem daunting to achieve balance under stressful conditions, but with practice we can consciously develop ways to achieve this state.

Developing Self-Awareness as a Tool

A powerful tool that we can use to practice achieving dynamic balance is the development of our self-awareness. This awareness can serve as a guide to our own personal truth and allow us to discern what our true needs are. This knowledge is important because it allows us to know when we are acting out of ego or desire or a place of truth. The goal is to enhance our ability to correctly understand our feelings and their source through self-awareness, so that we can make good decisions on how to take care of ourselves throughout our studies and in life.

Everyone possesses that inner voice or integrity that shouts at you when you need to take a break or slow down. It is only when we violate our integrity by existing too long in survival mode that we end up suffering. A good example of someone who listened to her feelings and kept her integrity was a friend and fellow medical student. She had just started a neurology clinical rotation when she realized that she needed a break. Overcoming a personal history of losing her mother, not knowing her father, being raped, and enduring foster care, she had powered her way through college. Similarly, she had tackled the first three years of medical school with rigor and focus. But suddenly, the demons of her past overtook her. Realizing that she could not complete this clinical rotation, my friend sought out the clerkship director, who was unfortunately not receptive to her situation. The director told her she could not take a break and must "tough out" the month-long rotation. Knowing her own needs clearly, even in the midst of a high-tide of emotions, my friend advocated for herself. "I am sorry, but I cannot continue this rotation. I'm going to take a month off to rest so I can get stronger," she said. The director was shocked—and furious that her power had been so usurped by my friend's clarity. She accused my friend of being mentally unstable and in need of psychiatric attention. She also told her that she would be a failure as a physician and intellectual. My friend, fully vested in her truth, calmly and respectfully replied, "Thank you for your opinion. I am sorry that we do not agree. But I will not take this rotation at this time because I need to take care of myself. Please sign these papers so I can turn them in to the office. Thank you." Unable to intimidate or control my friend, the director signed the papers. My friend successfully completed the neurology rotation months later, and entered the residency of her choice after medical school.

So how can we cultivate an increase in our self-awareness? The first step is through self-assessment—looking at ourselves as we are right now. By assessing our current situation, we can identify and develop a clear understanding of our areas of strength and weakness. One approach that we can use to assess our current situation is to find a calm, quiet place and actively ask ourselves probing questions. What am I doing? What am I not doing? What are my desires? What do I avoid? As you allow your mind to calm, what kind of thoughts reappear in your mind? Are they positive or negative? How are your relationships, and are they having an impact on you? When do you tend to harm or hate or sabotage yourself? What are your judgments, fears, and defenses? Are you carrying any unresolved grief? The answers to these questions will be our baseline measures of the person we are right now.

Once we know where we are starting, we can develop two more pictures of ourselves—as healthy and balanced or unhealthy and out of balance. By using the same assessment categories, we can brainstorm a list of qualities, symptoms, and indicators of either being balanced or out of balance. For instance, the following questions may help you with this process: When do you eat? When do you multitask? Do you "check out" of reality by using some distraction method like television? Do you numb yourself with substances like alcohol or drugs (including caffeine!)? Do you isolate yourself from or cling to the presence of others? Do you exercise? Do you talk about your feelings? As you create the three contrasting pictures of your present, balanced, and out-of-balance states, you can now use your self-awareness to practice balance.

Remembering to Balance

Sometimes certain skills that can be advantageous, like studying hard, can eclipse our search for balance. There was a movie released several years ago in which the main character was afflicted with short-term memory loss. In order to carry out his plans for revenge of an event he kept forgetting, he inscribed the event on his chest as a memory trigger. In many ways, this story resembles the selective amnesia that can be brought on by higher degree studies. We are so focused on factual data, new information, and studying that we forget ourselves. We forget our good intentions to take care of ourselves and look for balance. Often, people who are strong, smart, and successful only seek balance when life breaks them down through tremendous stress or grief. I have frequently noticed how people in higher degree programs will wait until they are grossly out of balance before seeking better strategies for managing their lives. A perfect example of this point was given in a keynote address by Oprah Winfrey in 1999. She described a pattern of realization that she observed many times. "It's like God starts out with a whisper in my ear, then a tap on the shoulder, then a punch in the arm, then a slap upside my head, and, if I still don't get it, there's this brick wall that I run into with my whole body." In order to prevent unnecessary suffering, we need to be proactive and implement a system of awareness triggers that will remind us of our intent to be and stay balanced.

The best awareness triggers come from knowing your personality and habits. For example, visual cues may work well with your personality, in which case you could hang a note on a mirror to remind yourself. Or you might respond better to a support system, where enlisting the help of your friends and family may help with your efforts to remember balance. In addition, committing to a group, meditation class, or individual counseling may be a way for us to remind ourselves of our efforts. Any method we choose will set us up to be successful as we embark on practicing balance.

After we have a system of reminders for our intent to be balanced, we need to examine our ruts. A rut is something we do over and over again out of habit and is thus relatively hidden from our awareness. These rutted patterns can destroy our efforts to practice balance. Therefore, we should take a moment to get to know them, like potholes in the road. We can see our ruts quickly by writing down what events or patterns cause us to lose awareness, ignore our own needs, or become complacent and lazy. On this list are the things that cause us to stop striving and even sabotage our system of reminders. It is sad but true that our worst enemy can sometimes be our own self. This list will be a safety net as we create an action plan for achieving balance.

A Balanced Plan

To review, so far we have taken inventory of ourselves, created pictures of our balanced and out-of-balanced states, set up a reminder system, and examined our ruts. Now we can create a plan of action that fits our unique needs and qualities. Keep in mind that a plan that we will actually use is the only kind of plan we want to create.

Step One: Know What Nurtures You

The first part of our plan is to make a list of methods or activities that feed us and most often bring us into balance with ourselves. These could include spending time in nature; spending time with a friend, pet, or partner; attending classes; reading self-help material; or engaging in creative arts. Whatever your preference, it is helpful for you to be aware of the entire menu of resources available for your self-care.

I've realized that by being open to many forms of healing and nurturing, I've discovered and healed things about myself that I never would have otherwise. For example, after a decade of intense study and work, I found myself getting tired early in the evening for no apparent reason. Knowing that Western medicine solutions were limited, I sought the advice of a psychologist who was recommended for an esoteric type of emotional release therapy using gentle tissue massage. Having had many years of sports massages, I was open and hopeful that this approach might help me. However, I had prejudice against psychotherapy from my childhood experiences with ineffective family therapists. Reluctantly, I started talking about my life as required in the workup for my massage therapy. After hearing my story, the doctor looked at me and said, "Well, you are burning out. You have a decision to make, because you have such a buildup of emotional weight. Either you make a firm commitment to go through and resolve this density of grief, or you will find that one day you won't be able to get out of bed." This news shocked me, since I thought I was in pretty good shape. However, we know the truth when we hear it, and I had just heard it. To my amazement, I went to see him every week for over a year. And in all that time, I never once did the massage therapy, but instead did regular psychotherapy. It was one of the best things that I have done for myself, and it was certainly one of the biggest investments in my health that I've made.

Step Two: Schedule of Self-Care

My mother was "on a diet" for approximately 60 percent of her life by my count. Ironically, as much as she would announce that she was starting her diet, I never heard her say when she was officially ending it. Sound familiar? In order to avoid the trap of setting non-sustainable expectations, we must be honest with ourselves about what our next step will be. This way, we slowly build momentum and control over our behaviors, which will work from our self-awareness to bring balance. The biggest mistake people make in initiating any changes in their behavior is impatience. We will be wise to first pick a target date to start and update our balance plan. The period of time leading up to this date should be short, to preempt our natural falling off, but long enough to allow us to get into our new behavior. Monthly plans work well for most people.

We will use the first day of each month as a start date, and we can draft a schedule and checklist of daily, weekly, and monthly nurturing activities or practices. These are things that we think we can do reliably, without needing regular reminders. A good way to position this schedule on our edge of growth is to ask ourselves, "What next step toward balance am I ready to sustain?" It is better to do one small thing for years than to have a complex, elaborate plan of total transformation that lasts only one week.

As we follow our plan, we should think long term. Fortunately, students in higher degree programs are very good at this. A monk once shared a story with me about visitors who came to the monastery looking for spiritual growth. After weeks of following the practices of the monastic, they would approach this monk and express frustration over their lack of progress. "Ah," he would reply, "be patient with yourself. Maybe if you keep practicing, you might see some improvement in twenty years or so." When it comes to the delicacy of balance, the release of ego, and expectations required to be balanced, we must be gentle. Better not to enrage our ego. We will likely see self-sabotage, resistance, avoidance, and other backlash behaviors if we push too hard or force ourselves beyond our natural next steps.

Step Three: Identify What to Avoid

After we have a manageable schedule for promoting balance and self-care, we can write down what we should avoid. Avoiding influences that move us away from balance may be necessary as we put our action plan into place. Looking at our list of distractions and symptoms of a lack of balance, we can see what people, places, or situations we may need to avoid. A recovering alcoholic needs strength to walk past a bar. Likewise, we are addicted to being out of balance and need strength to recover. Since my addiction was tied to overcommitment, I had to learn to avoid going to meetings, talking to certain people, or volunteering to help. Eventually, we will not need to avoid anything, because our practice of balance will be stronger than our addictions to being out of balance.

Step Four: Decide When to Be Counterculture

Special categories of things we should avoid but may not think to avoid are culturally embedded behaviors. Because everyone is doing it, these behaviors may be insidiously throwing us out of balance. For example, coffee is considered the "sacred cow" of Western culture. It is used as a drug to override the natural messages of fatigue or the need for rest sent by our body. And how can we practice balance if we are so out of synch with our needs?

Let's imagine for a moment that we are totally plugged into all culturally set behaviors. We would drink alcohol or smoke cigarettes or eat food if we were stressed—all the while joking about what a vice this is for us. We might also engage in romantic relationships or even sexual intimacy, even when we didn't really want to, because we were either lonely or fulfilling the expectations of others. We would wake ourselves up with coffee, keep ourselves up with coffee, and then put ourselves to sleep with some other drug. We would do whatever our professors asked just to impress them. We would shop and shop because we were bored or trying to fill an empty space inside. We would be at the mercy of pleasing friends and family at the expense of our own needs. We would engage in workplace gossip or depressing conversations about fear-provoking news stories. And we would soak in and participate in all of this without questioning any of it.

These are just some of the ways that we may become conditioned to fit into our world. Fitting in was not just a concern in adolescence;

clearly it still has power over us today. If we care what others think of us, then—to be balanced—we have to be clear about when and where we will break from the pack. Again, by being self-aware we will see our truth. This truth will show us when and where we will need to be counterculture. Writing down our intentions about when to be counterculture is the final piece of our action plan.

In Case of Emergency, Break Glass

Sometimes, no matter how thorough and compliant we have been with our own intent to balance our lives, everything falls apart. At these times, we must recognize two things: first, we are now in survival mode, and second, we must be extremely gentle, non-judgmental, and helpful to ourselves. Having some emergency backup resources and support is crucial. This may include creating an emergency call list, including professional mental health services.

If this period in your life is less severe and you feel it is manageable on your own, there are several methods you can turn to. Gratitude is a powerful antidote to mild depression and feelings of not having enough or not being enough. We can express gratitude through verbal or written appreciation for others or may simply keep a journal on all that we are grateful for. Patience is the antidote for anger and frustration. Practicing patience can include sitting silently for a few minutes, abstaining from multitasking, walking slowly, and eating mindfully (savoring each bite). Self-nurturing in the form of getting a massage, sitting in a hot tub, or taking a long nap may also be very helpful. However, we must be careful that these practices are truly nurturing our soul as opposed to merely being an escape (as shopping sometimes is). Communication with others may stem feelings of isolation and misunderstanding. Expressing one's feelings also may restore balance.

Finally, taking responsibility for one's life circumstances is an empowering way to endure such a period. Remembering that it was our own choice to be in a higher degree program can prevent our minds from indulging in a sense of victimization. May we be brave enough to take full responsibility for our own balance.

In Conclusion

Being balanced in life, let alone during an intense studies program, is challenging and fluid. We will never "get there," since balance is a process—like breathing. However, self-awareness, self-inventory, nurturing practices, and knowledge of when we are out of balance offer a comprehensive plan for us to see what we need and to pursue it. Since we can rarely alter our external world to give us perfect balance, our true balance will only come from within.

CHAPTER 3

Reaching Academic Excellence by Discovering Your Innate Learning Style

By Frederick L. Moore, Ph.D.

Introduction

Any student of science is expected to acquire, comprehend, and assimilate large amounts of information. The ability to understand how your mind processes information, stores it, and recalls it is a valuable tool that can empower you to excel in many areas of life. Since this understanding of the mind can benefit people who challenge themselves to reach new heights of mental awareness, at the end of the day, there is no limit or end. The results are a clearer consciousness of thought and a better understanding of your own learning process. The goal, however, is for our minds to forever evolve. So we have to be clear from the start that people experience life differently, perceive events differently, and process information differently. Nevertheless, we can gain much from understanding our learning process, and equally important, we can benefit from adapting our minds to understand other people's processes.

During my time as an undergraduate student, I realized that with each transition to an upper-division science course, I was required to retain information for a longer period of time. Each semester it became more critical for me to retain the information covered in the course from the previous semester. At this point, I knew that if I wanted to become a successful scientist, I needed to create a knowledge base that would last for an extended period of time. As I searched my mind for the most efficient ways to process and remember details, I also analyzed the minds of brilliant people with whom I came into contact. I wanted to understand how they figured out problems; I wanted to understand their logic. This approach allowed me to compare and contrast the way they understood and processed information to my own innate learning style. This chapter isn't a comprehensive look at how the human mind works, but rather a composition of tools and techniques that have helped me to diversify my problem-solving portfolio and develop mental confidence.

Mental Confidence

My definition of mental confidence is the ability to learn new information, utilize it, and be self-assured that you have applied it correctly. The development of this ability can enhance many areas of your life. For instance, I noticed that many students who learn information to take an exam have no idea afterward if they've passed the exam or not. I also noticed that many students can discover the answer to a problem, yet have no understanding of how they solved it, and can't explain the solution/process to anyone. I discovered that with a deeper understanding of my thought process, I was more comfortable relying on my stored information, I gained a greater sense of confidence when utilizing that information, and I could articulate my logic to my peers. I believe there are mental lines that are crossed that move one from "I understood the information" to "I can explain the information." Understanding a concept can be an unconscious process, but explaining a concept is definitely a conscious process.

One way to develop mental confidence is to develop a check and balance system within your mind. For instance, when you learn something to take an exam, the only person you can depend on at the time of the exam is you. So we have to learn how to be our own worst critic. That means we have to develop a system that constantly tests the information we are learning until we have proved to the system that we understand the information completely. The technique described below can help with the process of becoming conscious of the information that you store.

Interactive Reading

One ingredient necessary for excelling in science is the ability to critically read and analyze other people's work. As an undergraduate student, I took the information that I learned from books as the truth. In general, it seems like our society propagates the notion that people should not question the information that they learn in school and from books. It wasn't until I was in graduate school that I began to realize that the information presented in books could be outdated and sometimes incorrect. In addition, authors are sometimes biased as to what they believe is the truth, and that is what they write. For example, sometimes there are contradicting models of how a process works. If the author of a book believes one model over the other, the model that is favored by the author is presented in that book. And sometimes it is later discovered that the other model is more valid. Because I'm an inquisitive person, after I understood how information is presented in books, I was inspired to consciously challenge everything I read, which consequently made me a more active reader.

Interactive reading is the act of engaging the material that is being read as if you were having a conversation with it. During the course of the conversation, you form an opinion about the material that you are reading in the same way you form an opinion about information someone tells you. Basically, do you believe what the author is saying? When I studied alone, I used a multistep approach to reading. My first charge was to read a paragraph for understanding. I know this sounds simple, and you may be thinking that this is what everyone does when they read something, but I tried to understand the information from the same logic as the author. Thereafter, I would critically analyze the content of the paragraph and actively search for loopholes in the author's logic. For instance, understanding the author's logic when reading a paragraph is a passive process, and I mentioned earlier that the information isn't always stored on the conscious level. But the active process of thinking through each paragraph and looking for errors in the author's logic will help you to form your own opinion about the material. Lastly, I tested myself on the new information that I had just learned. After every other paragraph, I would ask myself questions about the previous paragraphs to see if I still remembered or understood the information. This stage in the multistep process is part of the check and balance system.

As a result of this quizzing process, I would make notes of the information that I did not understand, and I often noticed that the answers to my questions would be presented in the subsequent paragraphs. This interactive form of reading allowed me to recall information for longer periods of time because, in reality, I was having a conversation with the information in my mind, thus forming my own virtual study group.

This process to interactive reading might seem to take a lot of work, time, and effort. Basically, at first it does. However, I discovered that when I read interactively, I understood information better than my peers. I realized that I didn't have to go back and reread things three or four times. And in the final analysis, I also realized that my mind would automatically integrate all of the parts of the multistep process at the same time. So a person could view this process as an initial time-consuming investment, but the rewards are a powerful memory, mental confidence, and a conscious articulation of your thoughts and logic.

Start Discovering Your Innate Learning Style

Research has shown that people process information in different ways. Some people process information visually, where they utilize an image, drawing or picture to problem solve or understand information. Others are auditory learners, where they can recall something from a previous conversation and/or lecture and utilize that as a resource to problem solve. Many musicians and singers process information in this way. They have the ability to hear a song once and replay the song exactly the way they heard it or sing the song in perfect pitch. Lastly, some people learn kinesthetically (through feeling), where they can utilize their senses to place themselves in a situation to problem solve. For example, I am a visual and kinesthetic learner. When I studied organic chemistry, I would draw out a molecule and imagine, utilizing my senses, how the molecule would respond in a given chemical environment. This approach allowed me to be more intuitive about how molecules with unique properties (charges, etc.) would act or respond in a basic or acidic environment with other molecules.

Since we all possess an innate learning style, it is important to understand your process, because it can enhance your ability and efficiency to take in or absorb information. For instance, if you are learning a foreign language and your main way to process information is auditory, it may be easier for you to hear a word and remember its pronunciation (because of your audio ability), pronouncing it thereafter exactly as you first heard it. In contrast, people who process information visually may hear the word, but then need to have the word spelled for them, make a mental picture of the word, and later remember the details. My advice is to pay close attention to how you study. Do you tape record your lectures? Do you draw pictures of things you want to understand? When things make sense to you, does it feel right? Do you typically try to place yourself in other people's perspective when they are telling you a personal situation in order to understand them? Do you learn better from a book, or do you need to attend the lectures? These are all clues that can help you to discover your innate learning style. I discovered that after I understood my innate learning style, retaining information felt nearly effortless. I could educate people on the most effective way to teach me and/ or I could ask the right questions to learn something. In addition, this deeper understanding of self allowed me to transform/decode information from multiple sources into easily digestible pieces. Thus, one can see how understanding your innate learning style can further lead to developing mental confidence.

Enhance Your Memory—Instant Playback

If you weren't blessed with a photographic memory, don't feel lost; there is hope. Studies have shown that every thought or memory we have ever had is stored in our minds as a picture and that our minds have unlimited potential to remember pictures [1, 2]. Even if you are an auditory learner, your mind will remember where you were when you heard the information and link those thoughts back to a picture. When I was in school, I utilized a technique I called "instant playback" to remember the facts and details of scientific processes. I called it that because, in reality, I was making a subconscious movie of the information that I was learning. For instance, if I were trying to remember a five-step biochemical pathway, I would first focus on understanding the meaning of each step in the pathway individually. This process involved drawing out the different steps of the pathway on paper and creating logical connections between each step. Why does step A go to step B? If step B were absent from the pathway, what would happen to step C? By drawing out the steps and working through the logic that linked the steps together, I was able to create ties between the pictures and the information. This process allowed me to combine all of the pictures together from each step into one continuous movie. I realized later that when I needed to remember a detail about the pathway, I could replay the movie in my mind and stop at the step that I wanted to analyze. Amazingly, the logic that connected that step to the next step was still available! I believe that instant playback enhances your ability to remember details; and equally important, it allows you to store the information in your mind in an organized fashion.

Benefits of a Study Group

Some people believe that working in study groups is a waste of time; I would agree, if you don't have the right people assembled for it. However, if one utilizes a study group properly, it can be a powerful way to learn and develop mental confidence. For example, if you are the type of person who does not feel the need for a study group in order to excel in classes, my questions for you are: Can you articulate your knowledge to others effectively? Do you remember information for long periods of time after an exam? Can you learn information from others in a different style/ logic than yours? Can you effectively integrate other people's logic or problem-solving techniques into your natural way of thinking? If the answers to any of these questions is no, then you can benefit from a productive study group.

I believe that study groups should be formed in the same way that a coach puts together a basketball team—with careful thought and precision. Also similar to a basketball team, each player has to try out for a position. Each player needs to come to practice and remember his or her drills. And most importantly, when it is game time (exam time), each player must play to win. My first rule for a productive study group is to never study with folks who are not about their business. I don't mean that you should find people who are anal-retentive if you are not, because compatible personalities should be weighed into your equation. But find people who are responsible. My second rule is to have diverse minds represented in your study group. This rule is important because we now realize that people process information differently, and you want to study with people who have multiple approaches to problem solving. Lastly, if possible, don't choose people for your study group who are impatient and selfish. The last thing you want is for someone like that to rush other study members into saying that they understand something, when they really don't.

Participating in study groups while in college forced me to form opinions faster, remember information longer, learn alternate problem-solving approaches, and develop teaching skills. For example, I studied with a friend in college whose thought processes were totally different from mine. We would argue for long periods of time about why one approach was right compared with the other. We came to realize that oftentimes we were saying the same thing, but different frames of reference. I learned a lot from this person, because we could both obtain the same answer to a scientific problem and utilize two different approaches to solve it. I realized that when we would go back over our problems together and explain our approach and logic to each other, I could discover an alternate pathway to solving a problem that was more efficient than mine. But perhaps even more important, if I incorporated my friend's approach into my problem-solving skill set, I had more tools available to solve problems. This one extra step to learning allowed me to expand beyond my innate learning style, and I developed better conceptual problem-solving skills.

I think students need to study on their own first and exhaust their own mental resources before depending on someone else for help; however, students need to realize that it doesn't make a difference who helped them learn a concept or information before an exam, because that person's name will not be associated with the grade on the transcript. So, by developing a productive study group, you can further develop your ability to explain information and, at the same time, incorporate new problem-solving skills into your mental toolbox.

Visualizing Your Success

Many students have rituals and routines that they perform before they take an exam. I've had friends who would wear the same outfit each time, study in the same room the exam was being held, or designate a lucky mechanical pencil to use in order to feel comfortable in their surrounding environment. I believe these different routines can work for people, even if all they do is provide a certain level of stress release. The reality is that everyone experiences pressure differently when they take an exam, and they have to develop their own way to relax and retrieve information under these conditions. I'll share with you two techniques that I have helped me to keep my cool under pressure.

The lyrics to the song "I Believe I Can Fly," by R. Kelly speak to my mentality about overcoming obstacles in life; the lyrics say, "If I can see it, then I can do it. If I just believe it, there's nothing to it." My routine every night before an exam was to simulate a test-taking situation in my mind while I was falling asleep. This entailed visualizing myself in the classroom where I would be taking the exam and programming my mind for success. I would see myself taking the exam in my favorite chair and feel my mind knowing the answers to every question that I encountered. Yet with each test one takes, there is always drama before the completion of it. During the last five minutes of the exam, I would come across those one or two problems that I couldn't figure out, and I would practice telling myself that I knew the answer to those problems. I would feel the pressure mounting on me, because I knew that I was running out of time, but I would tell myself to calm down and relax, and move my mind to a distant quiet place. At this point, I would watch the lines of communication that signal information stored in my unconscious mind open up and send the needed information to my conscious mind. Afterward, I could feel that I knew the answers to the problems and I would see myself answer them correctly. So the next day, when I would be in the last stages of the exam and those few problems would arise that I couldn't solve, I would visualize myself relaxing and opening up the lines of communication in my mind—and the information would come. Interestingly, I have talked with other students about this technique, and I've realized that others have developed similar techniques to program themselves for success. For example, one friend mentioned that he boxed with a problem, as if he were in a boxing match, and he would watch himself defeat his opponent in his mind. Regardless of what your scenario is, this can be a powerful way to train your mind for success.

There was a period during my undergraduate career, shortly before I figured out the technique mentioned above, where I wasn't finishing my exams on time. I felt like I knew the information before the exam, but I couldn't recall the information in sufficient time to finish it. After much agonizing thought, I realized that I did better on exams when I had a practice test the day before. But more importantly, I realized that I did better when I had a timed practice exam. I began to understand that when I learned information in a relaxed setting, the information was easier to recall because I wasn't under pressure; however, when I was under pressure, I would often second-guess myself. It became clear to me that I had to prove to myself that I could remember and become confident with the information while studying in a relaxed setting, and then test myself with the timer before each exam. I think that many students face this dilemma. My advice is to use a stopwatch, timer, etc. and stimulate test-taking conditions. This technique allowed me to gain more mental confidence under pressure and become a better test taker.

In Closing

I believe that the most effective skill any student can acquire while navigating through college is to develop an understanding of his or her mind. Having a deep understanding of your innate learning style and a healthy appreciation for the diverse style of others can serve you well in the future. These skills are transferable in many areas of life, which include anything from giving a talk in corporate America to managing a team of diverse individuals with unique strengths and weaknesses to developing a powerful mind that can aid you when you encounter the pressures of life. At the end of the day, there is no limit to how powerful our minds are. Some of us place limits on the potential of our minds, but the people who manage to excel and overcome life's obstacles are those who always tend to find new ways to grow and push themselves past their preconceived limits. These accelerators at the game of life try to harness all of the power they possess. Even though the information I have presented in this chapter has helped me to elevate my mind, I am continuously searching for better ways to think efficiently and understand all parts of it. There are countless other techniques that can and will work better for you than these, but it is up to you to learn and develop them. My advice to you is to consider this information as a starting point in your quest to reach your mind's highest potential.

FOOTNOTES

[1] F.A. Yates, *The Art of Memory* (Chicago: The University of Chicago Press, 1996), 400.

[2] D.H.L.a.C. Prowant, *Mind Manipulation Ancient and Modern Ninja Techniques* (New York: Kensington Publishing, 2002), 181.

CHAPTER 4

The Five-Step Program for Preparing a Dynamic Graduate/ Professional School Application

By Michael L. Penn Jr., M.D., Ph.D.

Introduction

Applying to graduate or professional schools (GPS) can be an intimidating and daunting task. In my lifetime, I cannot remember a more stressful period. However, despite all the stress that it creates, this process is also an exciting opportunity for you to learn more about who you are and what motivates you. This chapter will describe five key steps that will help guide you along this incredible journey. Remember, it is all about your self. You cannot develop a strong application without a strong understanding of who you are and why you're applying to GPS. Therefore, the first step is to Know Yourself. The other steps—Love Yourself, Convince

Yourself, Apply Yourself, and Develop Yourself—follow in order. This chapter will challenge you to look deeper than you have ever looked inside yourself to uncover your true essence. It also requires that you let go of all the preconceived notions about what a "good" medical/graduate school application looks like. A winning application should reveal what makes you unique as an individual. The questions and tasks that you will be asked to consider in the paragraphs to follow will not be easy to complete, but you will reap huge rewards if you take the time to contemplate them completely and honestly.

First, you must realize that there are no magic tricks associated with gaining admission to medical school or graduate school. The practical information contained within this chapter can easily be found elsewhere. However, the specific perspective and approach that this chapter will offer you in terms of preparing for the process is unique. Hard work and solid grades and test scores are all very important, as one might expect. However, they represent only minimum criteria. Those students who take the time to introspect and challenge their assumptions and motivations about preparing a GPS application will be no doubt be most successful. It is my hope that you will be transformed and empowered by reading this chapter and that you will learn to believe in and celebrate your unique and innate gifts that relate to your future profession(s). This chapter is not a map. Each person's path is unique and this chapter is meant to highlight guiding principles for your journey to self-actualization. I hope you enjoy the ride.

Step One: Know Yourself

Having a thorough understanding of the kinds of experiences you want in life will help you enormously in preparing a stellar GPS application. Knowing what inspires and motivates you will provide a lens through which you can evaluate a variety of career opportunities. Find ways to articulate what experiences bring you joy, and learn how to create balance in your life. These activities lead to a more thorough knowledge of self and will provide you with a solid foundation upon which you can build a strong application. Self-knowledge will reflect in everything you do—including your GPS applications. It will make your personal statement come to life, your interviews entrancing, and your personality infectious. Think carefully about the questions below to begin this process. While they are by no means exhaustive, they offer a reasonable place to start learning about who you are and what moves you.

How would you like your career to make you feel? Fulfilled? Challenged? Exhilarated? Connected?

Do you feel more comfortable working in a team or as an individual?

How do you motivate yourself when your confidence is low?

What are your strengths (academic and personal)?

What aspects of your personality do you think might work against you being successful (personally, professionally, mentally)?

How do you deal with and overcome obstacles?

In what ways do you optimally receive and process information?

Are you confident with thinking independently?

Are you passionate about science and/or medicine?

Step Two: Love Yourself

This phrase has become somewhat of a cliché in recent years with the explosion of the self-help era. But despite its overuse, loving yourself is significant and will impact your life. Loving yourself does not have to be corny. It simply means knowing how to be kind and respectful to yourself consistently. In a state of self-love you tend to make decisions that are in your best interest, and you can forgive and accept your own limitations (like the grade you received on that challenging organic chemistry test last semester!). Hopefully, the following suggestions will ignite your new love affair!

Accept your imperfections.

Make choices for your life that are consistent with who you are as a person.

Always be kind to yourself.

Make efforts to claim success rather than failure.

View the mistakes you make as an opportunity to learn about and improve yourself.

Identify five things that you like about yourself and find ways to fall in love with them.

Make a habit of celebrating your successes. Keep a success log so that when times get difficult, you can recall your many victories over the years.

Be your own biggest fan.

Surround yourself with cheerleaders and coaches (people who will celebrate your success and give you advice to become even better).

Make no apologies for who you are. Develop the courage to be yourself.

If you are a minority student, be proud of your diversity. If you are an economically disadvantaged student, celebrate your ability to overcome the odds. If you have been afforded a plethora of opportunities, acknowledge your blessings and think about ways you can share them with others less fortunate.

Step Three: Convince Yourself

Before going through the process of convincing yourself about why you'd be an ideal GPS candidate, it is important to examine the real impetus behind your decision to apply. Given that the matriculation through GPS is long and arduous, it is critical that you are applying for the right reasons. Consider the statements below and see if any apply to you:

I am applying to GPS because I love science and there really isn't much else you can do with a science background.

I want to go to medical school because it is the most prestigious profession.

I want to go to graduate school because it is free.

I like being an achiever, and GPS represents the ultimate achievement.

I want to make a lot of money.

All of my friends are applying to either medical or graduate school.

My family wants me to apply, and I don't want to let them down.

I think I might not want a career in science or medicine, but I've invested so much into this already. I don't want to start over.

If some of these statements of motivation apply to you, then I'd recommend giving some serious thought to whether or not your motivations can sustain the extreme dedication and commitment that the rigors of GPS require. These "wrong reasons" are not necessarily exclusive criteria for success, but they indicate that your commitment to GPS may not be fully developed. I have seen several students who have applied based primarily on the wrong reasons. Two things tend to happen to this group: (1) they are not admitted because they don't submit convincing applications or (2) they are accepted to GPS but later find themselves laden with self-doubt and/or burnout because their commitment to GPS is not sufficient to carry them through the challenges of such academic pursuits.

What would you say to an interviewer who asks you very bluntly, "Why should we admit you into our university?" Not an easy question to answer on the spot. However, after going through Step 3 you will be able to answer confidently and specifically. Please take the time to answer the questions in this section. Write them down. If you cannot convince yourself that you belong in a GPS, how will you be able to convince an admissions committee? What is helpful here is to use your success log (see Step 2) as a starting point. Consider the following questions:

Why are you passionate about science and/or medicine?

How do you see yourself contributing positively to your future profession?

Have you worked hard to get where you are?

Are you appropriately prepared to start the application process? Where are your blind/weak spots?

Is your decision to have a career in science or medicine based on your unique talents?

Do you really believe that your grades and test scores ultimately determine how successful you will be in life? Or are there other dimensions that will propel you toward success?

Are you pursuing your own dream or someone else's?

What is it about the day-to-day aspects of laboratory research or patient care that appeals to you?

Take a good look at individuals in your chosen profession(s). Do you admire them and want to be in their company?

Have you considered alternative careers that might make you equally, if not more, happy? How did you rule them out ultimately and arrive at your decision to pursue GPS?

Are you prepared to make the financial sacrifices (high educational debt and/or low starting salaries) necessary for a career in science or medicine?

How have your experiences thus far prepared you for a GPS program?

Are you prepared for the possibility that you may not gain admission the first, or even second, time around?

Step Four: Apply Yourself

Many students who apply to GPS prepare their application in almost an automated fashion—like following a recipe from a cookbook. I would suggest that it be more like creating an original piece of art, something that tells a story about who you are. Unfortunately, competition for schools is so fierce that it creates an intense pressure to conform rather than stand out. Students rush to get laboratory experience and join clubs to prove that they're well rounded rather than truly developing themselves as individuals using their interests and passions as a guide. They then pack every detail of their lives onto an application without thinking about whether those items are woven together in a compelling way.

The decision to admit students never comes down to one grade, one letter, one publication, or one extracurricular activity. Understand that it is the composite of all your experiences that are evaluated. Therefore, it would be in your best interest to draw upon a wide variety of experiences (both direct and indirect) to tell your story. I have the hardest time convincing students that they need not worry about those few grades that are less than desirable—that they will be evaluated fairly. However, it's a fact that the students who trust their own instincts and avoid the competitive frenzy often navigate the grueling process quite smoothly and successfully. I have outlined below the major elements of the GPS application process and suggested a variety of ways to approach each one. Read on and apply yourself!

Academics

Focus on improvement of your weaker areas and consistency in your stronger ones.

Clearly explain and understand the reasons for suboptimal grade performance on your application. Communicate what you've learned as a result.

Develop means for long-term retention of knowledge.

Challenge yourself—take courses that will stretch your mind. Don't simply take easy courses that you will get As in.

Troubleshoot/reevaluate how to become a better student after every exam.

Extracurricular Activities

Don't just select activities because you think they will look good on your application. This will come across as superficial, insincere, and lacking commitment.

See that your extracurricular activities accurately reflect who you are.

Put your heart and soul into these activities (invest yourself).

Admissions committees like students who are leaders and take initiative. Think about creating an organization that is focused on your interests, and lead others to make a real impact in your school or community.

Admissions committees also like students who are team players. Think about a group that you can support passionately.

Have fun!

Understand that there isn't a right or a wrong choice in terms of selecting activities.

Think about activities that will allow you to make a unique and substantial impact.

Networking

Talk with as many people as possible who have gone through the process and learn from their mistakes and successes.

Get more comfortable with speaking about yourself in a positive way around others. Find ways to engage people in conversation so that they can learn what a great person you are.

Seek out and introduce yourself to GPS admissions staff/committee members in your area and schedule informational interviews with them. They possess a wealth of information and can give you great advice and insight long before you prepare your application.

Personal Essay

Begin preparing your essay at least a year in advance of the application cycle.

Have people from many different walks of life read it. This will give you a very balanced perspective of how well your essay represents you.

Make sure your essay answers the following question: "How will this profession enable you to fulfill your true purpose?"

Communicate your enthusiasm for this profession.

What adversities have you overcome? Sometimes the best way to get to know people is to understand how they respond to challenging situations.

Try not to list your accomplishments—integrate and weave them strategically into your personal story.

Start and finish strong. Make sure that if only the first and last paragraphs of your essay are read, they can stand alone and give compelling reasons why you should be admitted.

Letters of Recommendation

Write yourself a glowing letter of recommendation. Sometimes your references will ask how you see yourself.

Only submit letters of recommendation from individuals who feel they can write a strong letter for you.

Feel free to give your references an idea of particular personal attributes or accomplishments that you'd like them to highlight. This will help create a more compelling application.

Interview

Have an agenda. The interviews should not be approached passively. Think back to the things that convinced you in Step 3 and incorporate these into your interviews.

Learn how to find common interests and values between you and your interviewers and leverage those to build rapport and ease tension.

Don't forget that the interview is your opportunity to interview the school as well.

Practice!

Step Five: Develop Yourself (Conclusion)

Congratulations!!! You have finished the *Finding Your North* Five-Step Program. Successful admission into any graduate school or medical school is no small feat. The training and education you will receive will empower you to make meaningful contributions to the world. However, please remember that your journey does not stop with gaining admission. Please continue your self-exploration and keep your mind open to new opportunities to develop your skills and talents. Life has a funny way of carrying you wherever it pleases. By knowing, loving, convincing, applying, and developing yourself, you will always find happiness and fulfillment in whatever you do.

Section Two

Let Experience Be Your Guide: Personal Stories of Success and Struggle in Research and Medicine

CHAPTER 5

A Freshly Minted Ph.D.

By Alissa Myrick, Ph.D.

Introduction

On July 31, 2003, I defended my doctoral dissertation in front of four distinguished professors at the Harvard School of Public Health. After the examination ended, I waited outside of the conference room for a very long five minutes, and was welcomed back into the room as Dr. Myrick. Six years of work had led to that one moment; and it felt somewhat anticlimactic. The thesis defense consisted of an hour-long public seminar, followed by a closed examination in front of faculty. In other words, a one-hour scientific presentation was supposed to encompass four years of research. Years of effort were compressed into well-rehearsed, scientifically accurate, and concise points. What was filtered out? All the nights I stayed late in lab making sure my results were reproducible; all the hours spent waiting during incubations; and the exhilaration during the rare moments when I got an exciting result, when I discovered something totally novel, or when I remembered why I applied to grad school in the first place.

I learned many things during my journey through graduate school. I learned that the Ph.D. is about achievement, discovery, and sacrifice. Not only did I generate original data about a scientific question, but I also uncovered novel aspects of my personality such as my physical and intellectual limits, my strengths and weakness, and my ability to go beyond boundaries.

Choosing the Right Path

When I started my undergraduate career at UC Berkeley, I was sure of one thing—that I wanted to be a physician. My experiences over the next few years helped me to realize that this was not the right path for me. The first experience occurred while I was struggling through organic chemistry and physics and wondering when biology was going to show up on my course list. I started working as an undergraduate researcher in a lab that studied breast cancer. Once I was oriented to the lab techniques I needed to use, I found that I enjoyed my time in lab more than I did my classes. I think I was most excited by the whole aspect of the "chase" in scientific investigation. I enjoyed the challenge of coming up with good experiments in order to try and answer biological questions. The thought that I could "discover" something absolutely novel was exhilarating. I also realized the importance of biological research, and the opportunities there were to make significant discoveries that could benefit many people.

The second experience that shifted my path from medicine was my role as an HIV/AIDS peer educator on campus. I learned how powerful education and prevention can be in a community—that it is possible to slow the spread of a disease by transmitting knowledge. In essence, I learned the basic concepts that make up the field of public health.

The third pivotal experience of my college career showed me that sometimes we have to create our own paths. By my junior year, I was passionate about research and public health. I loved learning about AIDS because it is a disease that encompasses every aspect of life from the individual to the communal. A disease such as AIDS can only be stopped through multidisciplinary approaches. The summer after my fourth year of college, I was given the opportunity to witness the impact of this virus in sub-Saharan Africa. I worked at an HIV testing and counseling center that provided HIV/AIDS education to adults. It also had a research component, which studied the level of transmission among discordant couples. So there was public health and biological research, all while studying a health problem that had a huge impact on people of color. I realized that this was the type of work that I wanted to do, and that I had the skills and talents to make a contribution. This was certainly not an easy choice—being a doctor is something that everyone understands and the vast majority of people respect. However, one of the most important things I learned to do in college was to define things that I wanted to accomplish in life rather than to attach myself to a career. When I made my list of goals, I realized that going for the Ph.D. was the best path for me.

Applying and Interviewing

Once I made the choice to go to graduate school, I went about trying to figure out where to go and how to get in. You do not need to have your dissertation title in mind when you start applying to grad school, but you should have an idea of subjects that interest you. I started by making a list of topics that I thought were cool, finding out which graduate programs were researching those topics, and finally focusing on the professors doing that work. One way to start is by looking at scientific reviews. Take note of who authored the reviews—they will likely be scientists doing some of the most cutting-edge research in that field. You can look up journal articles authored by these professors as well. I made summaries of articles written by professors I thought I might want to work with; and I took those notes with me to interviews. When you are thinking about grad school, make use of the networks that you have. Ask your favorite science professor, teaching assistants, and grad students in labs you might have worked in if they know about the programs and professors you have selected.

Once you have been accepted to the program, you usually get flown in for interviews. This is as much a time for you to interview the program as it is for the program to interview you. Remember that finding the right graduate school is not just about the name and reputation of the institution. There is no point in entering a world-famous program if you find the majority of the research boring. Make sure that the program you choose is a good fit for your academic and personal needs.

One of the most informative things I did when I was interviewing was to ask the grad students how they were doing. I asked questions such as what the average time to finish was, if there was good career development in the program (for both academic and nonacademic careers), if students felt supported by the faculty, and if they felt like they were part of a community. I asked what the three best and three worst things were at every school I applied to. Finally, I asked grad students what their fellow students did after they graduated. Did they go on to successful careers? Did they leave science altogether? Did they ever come back to the program or become part of an alumni network? I tried to talk to numerous students, not just the cheerleaders of the programs; and, if I had the chance, I included students working in labs I was interested in.

All of the programs to which I applied were far away from my home in California, so I paid special attention to the cities and neighborhoods in which I could potentially spend the next six years of my life. Since I was contemplating big moves with big changes in weather, I also asked to speak with graduate students in the programs who had made similar moves to see how they adjusted. Do not be afraid to ask questions about those things that will make it easier for you to be a happy and functional human being in a rigorous academic program.

Grad School

When I started graduate school at Harvard, I was fully aware that as an African-American woman I was doing something special, something that my grandparents and all those before them had not had the opportunity to do. That was an important motivation for me. Find your motivation. Find more than one. Write them all down and keep that piece of paper in a safe place so that you can go back to that motivation during difficult times.

Classes

I thought that one of the most exciting things about going to grad school would be the opportunity to focus on the subjects that interested me, rather than wading through core requirements. That turned out not to be the case—usually you have to take a core group of classes. While I found that I was prepared for the workload, I was not necessarily prepared for all of the classes. For example, I didn't take immunology as an undergrad, so the grad-level immunology course was difficult for me. Don't be afraid to ask for help and get tutoring if you need it.

Grad school courses are often taught differently than undergraduate courses. The emphasis is on learning techniques and concepts that will benefit you in your research. One of the most significant skills I learned in these courses was how to read and critique journal articles. Scientific papers, not textbooks, are your knowledge base in research; therefore, it's really important to spend time learning how to read an article, analyze the figures, pull out the salient points, and identify possible weaknesses in the author's argument. Don't neglect classes, because those foundations will be important not only for your qualifying exam, but also for your research.

One thing I found during my first year at Harvard was that there were a lot of students who really wanted to impress upon others their vast knowledge and superior intelligence. There will be some geniuses in your classes, but there will also be a lot of posers. Find a group of supportive people you can study with. I found the study group I worked with during my first year to be invaluable. Not only did we help each other with course work, we also shared our experiences as we rotated through labs and sometimes even helped each other with experiments. I learned early on that it's important to form personal connections in science. Being part of a network of friendly grad students at Harvard provided me with a study group during course work, a critical peer group while preparing for my qualifying examination, accessible experts in various techniques and protocols, and interested and creative scientific intellects throughout grad school and beyond.

The Research Years

This is the most exciting and challenging time of your grad school career. You are going to develop a hypothesis and specific aims, and design experiments to address those aims. All of this work will generate original data that you will contribute to the field in the form of journal articles— and it will allow you to graduate. I had some of the best and worst times of my life during this period. One of the most rewarding aspects of this process was seeing myself develop into a better scientist, both intellectually and at the bench. The learning curve can be really steep but once you get over that hump, it's amazing how experiments can come together and you can start asking good questions. It's an awesome experience.

Joining a Lab

Of course, in order to do all of those fascinating experiments, you need to find a good lab to work in and a good adviser to guide you. Conduct an honest self-evaluation before you decide on a lab and an adviser. I wanted an adviser who could give me a lot of help at the beginning of my project, but would then relinquish control as I gained confidence and scientific maturity. I also wanted someone who was committed to graduating his or her students in a decent amount of time and who wouldn't let those students wallow around aimlessly in stalled projects. Once I had decided on the top two or three labs I was interested in, I spent a lot of time asking questions of the postdoctoral fellows and senior grad students in both of those labs. Since I had rotated in the labs, I had a sense of how each lab environment was, but I learned that it was important to go back and spend a little time in the prospective labs as a visitor, not as a rotation student. Joining a lab is a huge decision, filled with a lot of variables. Realize that there is no such thing as an ideal adviser, but try to find one who fits your profile fairly well.

Student/Adviser Relationship

The biggest challenge I faced with my adviser was learning how to present my ideas in a way that would be taken seriously. At first it seems silly to express a different opinion from a tenured faculty member who has decades of scientific experience and is a leader in the field. However, there's a danger of your project becoming the adviser's rather than your own if you don't. I'm also fairly shy. I would find myself walking into my adviser's office with a dozen half-formed, tentative ideas, and then getting inundated by detailed suggestions. One trick I learned was to write down my ideas and what I wanted to get out of every meeting and to show that paper to my adviser when we met. I stopped doing that as I gained more confidence, but it really helped at the beginning.

I had a professional relationship with my adviser. This generally worked well, but there were times during my research when I needed more than advice on how to troubleshoot failing experiments. At these moments, I would turn to my network of friends and family for support and encouragement. It is so important to have friends both outside and inside graduate school. My friends inside grad school were great for venting about research, learning new techniques, borrowing equipment, and talking about science. My friends outside grad school were great for escaping the lab, staying in touch with the real world, and keeping up with other interests. It's amazing how a one-hour lunch with a good friend can turn an entire week around.

Doing the Research

Everyone's thesis project takes shape differently. Some people get key results early on, and then struggle later. Other people have a slow start, great data in the middle, and then a lull at the end. I was one of those people who had a painfully slow start for the first two –and a-half years in my thesis lab, eventually reaching a crisis point. All of my major experiments stalled, and I could not find an experimental method to get around the problem. Then, for whatever reason, things started working, and I consistently got interesting data for the last one –and a-half years. Some of my best data came in the six months before I started writing my dissertation. During the period of crisis, I seriously considered withdrawing from the program. I felt like I wasn't making any scientific progress at all, I was wasting my adviser's money, and I certainly wasn't getting any closer to the Ph.D. Not to mention the fact that I was totally disillusioned with my project by that point. Somehow I managed to crawl over that wall—and I say "crawl" because it was slow and painful. If you're looking for amazing "Eureka! I'm a genius!" moments, you might want to flip to another chapter! I worked on smaller side projects that were working and could generate data pretty easily, and was gratified to see my lab notebook filling up. Meanwhile, I kept plugging away at the set of experiments that had stalled. I tried alternative techniques; I talked to people at conferences; I got advice at lab meetings; and finally, I got a result that satisfied my adviser, my committee, and me. Throughout these years, I had friends who were publishing papers and giving talks at major conferences while I kept presenting posters and dreaming of writing a paper. It could be pretty disheartening, and I guess if I look back, I would have started some of those side projects earlier. But it's hard to predict the biology.

Collaboration

I discovered the benefit of scientific collaboration late in my graduate school career. Collaboration is the scientific equivalent of a group project. A group of scientists from the same lab, or from different labs, get together to work on specific aspects of one project. Collaborations are important both on a scientific level and a social level. On the scientific level, working in a team allows you to look at your project from a lot of different angles and design complex experiments. The more hands working on a project, the more experiments that can be done, and the more likely you'll get really interesting (and publishable) results. I found that I worked harder during my collaborative work, because I didn't want to let anyone down. Also, I felt that there was much more creative energy during the collaboration. If I felt burnt out, somebody else would come up with an interesting question. On a social level, establishing contacts and a good reputation in different laboratories can only help you in your career. Of course, just like working on a group project, there can be drawbacks. It's important to make sure that everyone's priorities are clearly defined. For example, if one member of the team is working on the project for a thesis chapter while another member has been volunteered by their principal investigator (PI), the level of commitment may be different. Also, the authorship ladder should be established early on in the collaboration.

Publication

One of the things I wish I had done differently as a grad student was to try and frame my research in terms of a group of stories that could be bundled into manuscripts for publication. I think I was somewhat naïve in thinking that everything would fall into place and magically become a quality scientific article. The truth is that it is important to establish a solid publishing record. As you design your experiments, think about the figures you would want to see in a paper. Think of all of the control experiments you might need to do to confirm the accuracy of your data. Learn to discuss your project in terms of its scientific potential as well as its publishing potential. This is a place where your adviser and your committee can be really important, as they have experience in publishing as well as reviewing articles. Be careful not to let the thought of a paper drive your research, but realize that this is a key aspect of scientific research. Also, the more manuscripts you submit, the easier it will be to write your dissertation.

Lab Dynamics

Take one small group of highly intelligent and motivated people, place them in a small space, give them numerous tough scientific projects, and what do you get? Drama. The people who make up a lab end up becoming a highly specialized dysfunctional family. There were times during grad school when I spent more time in lab with my colleagues than I spent at home. As a result, I formed really strong bonds with the people I liked—and the exact opposite with the people I disliked. Professionalism is really important when working in a lab. Even if you have nothing socially in common with a fellow lab member, you can still maintain a constructive working relationship if that person has similar attitudes about science. I learned that antagonistic relationships in lab are some of the most exhausting and unproductive aspects of research and are to be avoided at all costs. It is no fun to dread going to lab because of the tension awaiting you there.

Personal relationships are one thing, but I think the most perilous situation is when your research is negatively impacted through the actions or inaction of a fellow lab member. Be wary of lab members, or anyone, who are interested and excited about your data but never shows you theirs. Be wary of people who offer to help you, but never really do. Take note of lab members who are willing to take the credit for exciting results, but aren't willing to do the grunt work. Observe everything before and after you join a lab.

Achieving Balance

I think the toughest thing about grad school is not knowing when you're going to finish. The data and your thesis committee decide that. Sometimes I felt like I was stuck in this seemingly endless process of doing experiments and trying to generate enough solid data to finish while all of my friends outside of grad school were moving beyond me into their real lives. I don't know how many times I would flinch when a well-meaning friend whom I hadn't seen in a while would ask, "Are you still in grad school?" That "still" could be the most depressing word in the world. What I realize now is that grad school *is* real life. It's the life you've chosen, and you've got to spend those years as fully as you can.

I tried to maintain a relatively balanced lifestyle by staying involved in activities I felt passionate about. In fact, one of the reasons I joined the lab I did was that I admired the diverse outside interests of the lab members. Face it, if you want to graduate, you won't be able to dedicate twenty hours a week to extracurricular activities, but you can pick and choose those things that keep you sane and healthy and spiritually nourished. I got heavily involved in various groups and was active in the social activities of my graduate program. I also developed a network of friends outside of science and made an effort to go to the occasional movie, club, concert, or art exhibit.

I learned a couple of important things from these efforts. The first is that once you get labeled as an active and engaged student, it's very hard to escape that. After a couple of years of good school citizenship, I reached a point where I was getting asked to organize events and activities because of my reputation for doing a good job. The problem was that I no longer had the time to do everything, because my experiments were becoming more time-consuming. Grad school is ultimately a selfish time. It's easy to get sucked into a bunch of activities, especially if experiments aren't going well in the lab. I learned to volunteer only for the things that I truly cared about and had time for. This meant going from being the co-chair of an organization to only participating in a couple of outreach events the next year because lab was demanding so much time.

The second lesson I learned was how to manage my time in lab so that I could have a life outside of it. I was in a serious relationship through most of grad school; about halfway through, my boyfriend moved to New York City, and we started a long-distance relationship. It became a priority for me to have about two weekends a month free, so I started planning my experiments weeks in advance and I would work extra hours during the weekdays so that I could hop on a bus on a Friday night with minimal guilt. I would do the same thing when I planned to go on vacations during grad school. Time management is essential.

Final Thoughts

Everyone's experience in grad school is different. If I stand back and look at my experience objectively, I would say that I had a fairly standard graduate school career. "Fairly standard" means that there were times when I thought I could not finish. It means that there were days when I forgot why I was there in the first place. The thing is, this monumental journey can be broken down into a couple of parts. The first is learning about the beast known as "scientific research." Months of work, even years of work, may end up being one figure in a journal article. Research takes time. The second part of the journey is learning about what it takes to be a good scientist. It's more than learning how to design an elegant experiment with all the right controls. It's more than learning how to ask a good question. You learn how to interact with people, how to work in a team, how to manage your time. You learn about the sacrifice it takes to be one of the best, you come to understand the politics behind the data, and you see the true face of science. This is what grad school is about. It's not easy, and it's not always fun. Only you can decide if it's worth it. Was it worth it for me? I started graduate school with the goal of gaining skills in molecular biology that could be applied to public health problems. My major focus was on infectious diseases, and I felt especially passionate about those diseases that are killing millions of people around the globe. Today, I am using my molecular biology skills and my understanding of public health concepts to study how the parasite that causes the disease malaria becomes resistant to drugs. I am not only studying the intricate molecular details of the parasite, but I am also looking at the parasite in relation to the population of people who are at risk for getting infected. Most importantly, I'm working with a team of people who have diverse ways of attacking this problem: physicians, nurses, epidemiologists, biostatisticians. All of us are working to find better ways to treat malaria, educate people about malaria, and understand how the parasite works. So all those late nights in lab? Yes, they were worth it.

CHAPTER 6

Learning to Set Sail: My Experience of Graduate School

By Tanya Henneman, Ph.D.

During the time I was a graduate student, two students and one former student committed suicide in the building that housed my office, a ten-story, gray, concrete building on the north side of campus. Two died by jumping off the building from one of the top floors, and the other by asphyxiation, tying a plastic bag around his head in the privacy of his office. As I was in the throes of graduate school, experiencing depression and a great deal of stress, these events affected me deeply. I understood that place inside of them that yearned for a release from their physical existence. However, such thoughts would be tempered by the words of my high school sex ed teacher, who told us more than once that suicide was a selfish act.

As a child and as a young adult, my life was plagued by much instability. Surrounding me were drug and alcohol addiction, domestic violence, mental illness, and interactions with a cold and dispassionate prison and legal system. As a consequence of these events, I became fearful and angry, but mostly I was sad after experiencing so much heartache in witnessing the people I loved self-destruct. These emotions were so overwhelming that I developed a coping mechanism that allowed me to get up each morning and move through my day as if everything were fine. I detached emotionally, focused on operating only from my mind and doing well in school. My life was compartmentalized to such an extent that I ceased having emotional reactions to anything, and I was so disconnected that I often felt I walked around in a fog, with no one able to really see me.

Berkeley, California is my hometown. It is a college town where the political-intellectual way of life reigns supreme across an eighteen-square-mile area overflowing with cafes and bookstores. Growing up, my strategy to focus primarily on developing my intellect was consistently validated in this academic culture and thus reinforced as a positive way to interact with the world around me.

This out-of-balance approach toward life and toward the learning process continued into college. With the encouragement of a professor, I decided to major in mathematics. Much of the appeal of mathematics lay in the certainty of answers and the unchanging logic used to derive a solution to a problem. During college, I felt pretty safe with this limited understanding of mathematics, finding pleasure in solving math problems, learning how to better organize my thoughts, and acquiring the skills to think more critically. There were moments in college when I felt the weight and pain of my past creep to the surface of my consciousness, and during these times I would want to isolate myself from other people, feeling ashamed and insecure about what I had experienced as a child. I didn't want to share myself or what I was experiencing, whether it was positive or negative, with anyone. Usually, I pushed these moments away by focusing on my studies, remaining in denial about the need for an emotional release. The recognition I received for my talent in math validated me, while tutoring and mentoring others helped me to feel I had something of value to contribute. There was no real incentive for me to change or to address what was going on in my life. My coping mechanism allowed me to not only be functional but highly successful—until I got to graduate school.

One immediate challenge to my way of thinking and learning came about because of my choice to study applied mathematics and later biostatistics as opposed to pure (theoretical) mathematics. Biostatistics is the application of statistical methods to biological and medical problems. I became intrigued with this field because I had an interest in public health, and biostatistics became a way of blending my background in mathematics with medicine. This discipline was different from the traditional math I had previously studied. When unraveling mathematical proofs in college, I could be logical and detached from the conclusions. To me, solving math problems was tantamount to nothing more than executing mental exercises. Learning biostatistics forced my mind to expand in a new direction. Decisions and results stemming from a biostatistics-related project often have a direct consequence on the health and well-being of real people. There is rarely an exact or right answer to a problem, because statistics is all about measuring and interpreting uncertainty and variability. In addition to understanding the mathematical concepts behind statistical models and tests, I had to be creative, opinionated, insightful, and responsible for my conclusions. That was one strain on my way of thinking.

During college, my estimation of my analytical approach to life was that it was a fairly successful one, and one that was consistently affirmed and validated by my teachers and peers. However, once I began graduate school, even though I still experienced a lot of the positive encouragement I was used to, I was also confronted for the first time with negative misperceptions from other students and faculty about my ability to thrive in an academic environment. During my first year of graduate school, I remember feeling shocked after walking into a graduate-level math class and being told that I must be in the wrong classroom, and that the French class I was probably looking for had moved to another room. That same year, a fellow student told me I was sure to pass my prelim exams (those you take to advance from a master's program into the doctorate program) since I was an African-American woman and the department needed to diversify its student population. And after my first semester of doing fairly decently in my classes, one of my professors told me during the midyear review that he and the faculty were surprised at how well I had done; until that moment, I never realized they had admitted me with low expectations. These experiences are not unique to me, and are not uncommon among women or people of color in the sciences— and, compared with some, they were fairly minor and innocuous. But they affected me in the sense that I had become dependent on the feedback of others, and every negative comment became integrated into my own perception of my capacity to learn and to achieve my goal of obtaining a doctorate.

By now, my approach to problem solving was being challenged and I was questioning my ability to succeed academically. But the greatest failing of my coping mechanism was that it left me unprepared to manage the emotional rigors of graduate-level study. The amount I was expected to learn and comprehend was amplified, the workload increased dramatically, and the pressure was intensified. Because I attached so much importance to my intellect, my time in graduate school translated into a seamless integration of my academic performance—as measured by qualifying exams, tests, the opinions of my professors and peers—with my sense of self-worth. My outlook on life became so distorted that every meeting, every exam, every report translated to a potential judgment of my significance. So many emotions had been bottled up inside me for so many years that I didn't have room for the additional stress, pressure, and fears of failure that I was experiencing. I was being pushed to maximum capacity. I wanted to cry and I wanted to scream, but I didn't know how to let go. And instead of finding a way to release and unburden what I felt, I kept internalizing it, I kept isolating myself, and I kept hiding. I sought refuge in my mind, shutting out those around me. This over-identification with the mind caused a loss of perspective and an experience of disconnection so severe that I could at times understand the desire to take flight from ten stories high on an otherwise beautiful day. Something had to change. If I was going to finish the doctoral program, I needed to understand what was happening with me. One morning, on the way to my office, I spotted on the ground a single page from a desk calendar. The date on the page was February 5, my birthday, so I picked it up, assuming it was for me. On the paper was a quote by William Shedd: "A ship in the harbor is safe, but that is not what ships are built for." I was that ship in the harbor.

Once, my logical, rational, and unemotional approach to engaging life had enveloped me as a protection against being hurt, judged, or exposed, but now it was holding me captive. The stress and pressure of graduate school was forcing emotions to surface that I didn't know how to express. Too much of my self-esteem was tied into my academic performance, and I had to discover a new and authentic source of validation. Not sharing who I was with others, shielding and isolating myself, was becoming more painful than protective. My way of coping with trauma had served its purpose, but now I knew I wanted and needed more from life. I was a ship in the harbor now ready to set sail. But now I had to learn how to chart a new course for my life.

My coping mechanism of not expressing emotions was not holding up under the pressure of graduate school; I had to reprogram how I dealt with stressful situations. First, I had to learn about what would trigger me to shut down emotionally, and what events would cause me to have a distorted perception of my worth and my abilities. To explore this, I sought individual and group counseling, where I learned about the effects of growing up around drug and alcohol addicts, and about being a witness to abuse. I began to realize that for most of my life, I had been operating in survival mode. To learn about other modalities of experiencing and living life, I became a voracious reader of spiritual, religious, and philosophical texts. What I learned inspired me to develop a meditation practice; to explore the power of prayer; and to spend more time in churches, temples, and in nature. To facilitate the release of difficult and painful emotions, I took advantage of my journal. Since the third grade I have kept a journal, and during graduate school this became a safe way for me to express my fears, doubts, and dreams. Finally, to remind myself of the skills I had to offer, I started a tutorial program with my sister for the youth in our old neighborhood. Through this program, I was able to reexperience what initially drew me into mathematics, and that was being able to help others. This experience reaffirmed that I had something of value to contribute to my community.

As I was learning how to defuse the role my coping mechanism played in my learning and creating process, I also took a couple of practical steps toward completing my dissertation. An essential element in this process was my participation in a dissertation study group that met weekly. Alongside a group of other African-American women, all from different departments, my dissertation was written in libraries, living rooms, and cafes. With each meeting I received vital moral and emotional support that kept me motivated and on task. Drafts of my dissertation chapters were shared with my study group and with other peers in my department for constructive feedback. With each revision my confidence grew, and I became more certain that I would be able to write a dissertation. During my last couple of years in graduate school, I became involved with activities in the creative arts that reminded me of the person I was outside of the academic environment. Becoming more   at ease with creative self-expression translated into greater comfort in recording my thoughts and ideas as they related to my dissertation topic. Finally, and most importantly, I surrounded myself with people who believed in me, encouraged me to succeed, and reminded me of what was truly important in life.

Part of my desire to travel down the academic path was in retrospect an erroneous belief that I could live my life solely from the mind, and all the hurt, sadness, and anger I experienced as a child and young adult could be neatly boxed away and stored on a shelf to sit quietly and collect dust. Thankfully, graduate school proved to be another experience entirely. In addition to gaining new skills, meeting amazing people from all over the world, and having an excuse to buy school supplies every year, the consistency of the academic year and the resources available at a large university gave me the time and space to focus on healing, which allowed me to withstand the pressure of graduate school and complete the doctoral program. The journey in the pursuit of knowledge is an amazing one, one that I plan to continue for all the days of my life. But I understand now that my rational mind is not all of who I am, and that my life must consist of a balance between my emotional, intellectual, and spiritual states. Each of us was born to share our own unique gifts and talents with our family, friends, and community. So just as it is selfish to take your own life, it is selfish to not share all of who you are—in essence, it is the same action. Let us set our sails and venture out of the harbor! The world is waiting!

CHAPTER 7
Graduate School and the Road Less Traveled

By Chad Womack, Ph.D.

It was the best of times, it was the worst of times, it was the age of wisdom, it was the age of foolishness, it was the epoch of belief, it was the epoch of incredulity, it was the season of Light, it was the season of Darkness, it was the spring of hope, it was the winter of despair, we had everything before us, we had nothing before us, we were all going direct to Heaven, we were all going direct the other way.... — Charles Dickens, *A Tale of Two Cities*

When I consider my experiences in medical and graduate school, the introduction to Charles Dickens' classic, *A Tale of Two Cities*, immediately comes to mind. I found both experiences to be challenging to say the least, each for their own reasons; however, I also found that it was the manner in which I entered those experiences that ultimately made the difference for me. My experiences in medical school challenged me to be honest with myself and to really identify my innermost desires and motivation for wanting to be what I perceived everyone else wanted me to be—a medical doctor—versus being what I wanted to be—a scientist. Similarly, my experiences in graduate school were unique and like no other academic experience I had encountered. The graduate school experience was unique in its ability to test endurance, patience, commitment, and dedication, and to bring out the best of one's passion for science and intellect, and, at times, the worst of one's insecurities and doubts. In medical school, I found myself asking why I was *really* there. Had I forsaken my real passion and love for science and research for a false sense of security that the M.D. profession would provide? Questions like that one would be by far some of the most difficult and personally challenging questions that I would ever have to face, and yet answering them would ultimately be the liberating force that would rescue me from the narrow confines of the self-imposed and false expectations that had limited my ability to grow personally and professionally.

By the end of my second year in medical school, I remember thinking that I was a complete failure. I was ashamed of myself for not doing as well academically as I thought I should. I began to judge my self-worth based on my appraisal of my fellow classmates while at the same time, somewhat unconsciously, I was waging an internal struggle in an attempt to answer the question of why I was in medical school in the first place. I felt the crushing weight of expectation of my family, my alma mater (Morehouse College), and my community. I felt I was letting everyone down. I felt that to even consider leaving medical school was a selfish act and would reflect poorly on everyone who had helped me to get that far. I remember thinking at that time: "How can I leave medical school when everyone is so proud of my being here and becoming a doctor?" I would be the first one in my family. I remember the pride that would exude from my grandmother as she would explain to anyone who would listen how proud she was of her grandson, the one who was going to be a doctor. I remember feeling how I wished I could just simply disappear.

Despite all of that, I knew by the end of my second year that I needed to leave medical school for my own sake. I realized that I had gone to medical school not because I really wanted to be a physician but because I mistakenly thought it would be the practical and sensible thing to do. I had made that decision in my senior year of college, before having explored all of my options. And given the choice between medical school or graduate school, I decided upon medical school, just like most of my premed classmates at Morehouse College. So off to medical school I went, not realizing that, for the sake of practicality, I would be sacrificing my true desire and relinquishing my life's passion, which was the pursuit of truth through scientific inquiry. As I left medical school, emotionally and spiritually bruised from having battled with the school's administration over the terms of my departure, I found myself struggling to redefine who I was and who I wanted to be as a human being, not just as an academic professional. I realized that in those two years of medical school, I had lost touch with the spiritual side of who I was, and ironically it was that side that was fighting and struggling to come out, struggling to be acknowledged against an indifferent academic environment that medical school provided.

Although it was difficult, leaving medical school gave me that much-needed space to rediscover who I was. It forced me to become reacquainted with my spiritual values and priorities. While it was a difficult and painful exercise, I began to realize that by putting myself in a narrowly defined box of professional identity (Chad the M.D.), I had allowed my experiences in medical school to almost destroy my inner self, my sense of self-worth and value. I had allowed an institution and a profession to define who I was and, even worse, to define my priorities rather than defining those things for myself. Truly there was and is nothing wrong with being a doctor, but in my haste to get to the next rung in the academic ladder, I had forgotten that my true love was for research and being a scientist involved in discovery.

Once I left medical school, it was clear that my first task would be to unlearn all of the negative thinking that I had developed as a result of those difficult experiences, and to begin to connect with my inner self and see what I was about. This would not be easy but, as the Dickens' quote articulates, "It was the best of times, it was the worst of times..." Part of what was "the best of times" for me was meeting my life partner and soul mate. She exudes a spiritual warmth from which emanates unconditional love and support; these qualities gave me strength during one of my most difficult times. Our friendship was the anchor I needed that allowed me to weather the storms of self-doubt brought on by the changes in my life. It also provided me with the much-needed space in which I could rediscover who I really was and reconnect with my life passion and dreams.

The process of healing from my medical school experiences would also be "the best of times" for me spiritually, as I would come to realize that the challenges medical school presented to me (be they academic or otherwise) were actually opportunities for me to learn about myself and to grow. Instead of looking upon them as moments of defeat, I began to see those experiences as spiritual battles that I had to wage against the dragons of failure and hopelessness—battles that would teach me valuable life lessons about who I was and lessons that I hold dear to this day. What I learned from my experiences in medical school was to not define myself by a particular profession and to not assess my value or humanity through institutional lenses, but rather to see myself as a spiritual person whose value and self-worth could not and should not be constrained by the academy.

As I began to heal the deep wounds of disappointment, I would recall those moments in my life when I had clarity about what and who I wanted to be. I would recall my high school years and how I would spend hours in the library reading everything I could about human cell biology and cancer. I remember clipping articles out of *Scientific American* journal and creating my own annual review of those that focused on any aspect of cancer. At that time, the biomedical research world had heralded the discovery of so-called cancer genes, or oncogenes, and the newspaper headlines were often filled with bold prognostications of cancer's imminent demise at the hands of the newfound science of oncogenes and the discoveries in cancer biology. The thinking at the time was that given the discovery of these aberrant genes, the next logical step was to correct them via gene therapy. Surely if we could identify the gene, we could fix it by replacing it with a healthy gene, one that didn't have the characteristic mutation associated with malignancy. Or, perhaps, with the new science and medicine, we could figure out ways to silence the bad ones...

As a high school student and someone whose curiosities were piqued by this new science, I had become fascinated with the prospect of becoming a scientist who would discover new cancer-causing genes and develop novel ways to fix them. In addition to this new science of oncogenes, virologists were discovering viruses caused retroviruses, which also caused cancer. Like a librarian shelving a new book in the library of the human genome, these viruses were unique in their ability to integrate their genomes into human cells, often causing them to become cancerous.

What I didn't realize at the time was how important my interest in cancer biology and, even more importantly, gene therapy would become in helping to shape my future interests in HIV/AIDS research and launching my graduate studies in human retroviruses. After leaving medical school and returning to the "bench" (as scientists call it), I began work as a research assistant in a lab that was focused on leiomyosarcomas, or what are known as fibroid tumors. While usually benign, these are tumors that disproportionately affect women of color, causing endometrial pain and discomfort, sometimes even uterine cancer. Working in this lab gave me a renewed sense of purpose and direction. It also provided me with the opportunity to begin to rekindle the flame for pursuing further study in graduate school, and in the following year I enrolled in a Ph.D. graduate program at the same institution. I had fully expected to continue to pursue cancer research as part of my graduate school training; however, I would soon discover how my passion for science and research would blend with my desires to connect that science with public health and help combat infectious disease worldwide.

It happened one day while attending a seminar presented by a professor from the Harvard School of Public Health. What he described during his presentation was absolutely fascinating from a scientific perspective and almost horrifying from the perspective of public health. His presentation concerned how the HIV/AIDS pandemic, caused by a retrovirus known as HIV, had begun to wreak havoc on the African continent, resulting in significant deaths in several nations. In slide after slide, he showed how HIV infection rates had risen to levels that were alarming in some countries and how, despite efforts to contain the virus, it had continued unabated, infecting mothers and then their children during childbirth. He then described the biology of this retrovirus in some detail, and described how the research in his lab at Harvard was helping to elucidate how this virus worked, the cells it preferred to infect, and how many variants of the virus are created because of random mutations generated by its replication machinery. Like Saul of Tarsus (Paul the apostle), who was blinded by the light, by the end of the professor's talk, I knew exactly what I wanted to do and be and why.

Here was HIV/AIDS, a serious scientific and global health challenge that was disproportionately affecting African peoples, and there was no treatment (at the time, in the early nineties, there was only one drug available—AZT), no cure, and no vaccine. It was clear that there was a huge scientific need for people like myself who were passionate about science and biomedical research to become involved in the field, to help fight against this deadly foe. All at once, I realized that what had perhaps been a rather tortuous route to graduate school was actually meaningful, since I would utilize some of my previous medical school training and education to inform the questions that guided my research at the bench. In addition to pursuing more basic questions designed to elucidate the fundamental HIV virology, I became fascinated with understanding how the virus' ability to mutate enabled it to evade effective antiviral therapy and the body's vigorous immune response. Simply put, the combination of my passion for science, public health, and compassion for others was the spark that reignited my flame and gave me my raison d'être—to be a scientist working on HIV/AIDS.

I have carried that passion ever since, and upon completing my Ph.D. in biomedical sciences at the Morehouse School of Medicine, I continued to focus my attention, both inside and outside the lab, on HIV/AIDS within African diasporic communities. My graduate work at Harvard and Morehouse gave me valuable insights and provided rather unique experiences in this country as well as abroad, allowing me to bear witness to the public health devastation that HIV/AIDS has wrought globally. I now routinely collaborate with African scientists who are facing the burden of HIV/AIDS in their countries. This has been extremely rewarding to me, as I am able to utilize my scientific expertise to assist in the global effort to develop more effective antiviral therapies and vaccines with the ultimate goal of eradicating HIV. Outside the lab, I am fortunate to be able to participate in more local efforts toward HIV/AIDS prevention. As a board member of two nonprofit organizations dedicated to HIV/AIDS prevention, I am blessed with the opportunity of working with truly phenomenal people who, despite having to deal with their own HIV status, are able to inspire others to join in the struggle against HIV/AIDS in the African-American community.

What I learned from the difficult and challenging experiences I had while in medical and graduate school has served me well in maintaining a perspective on what's ultimately important—pursuing my life's passion. I have been fortunate to have had great opportunities come my way, and I have also had the foresight to take advantage of them when they arrived. My experiences in medical school, although difficult and at times painful, would eventually turn out to be important in helping me to understand the science of HIV/AIDS and ultimately shaping the types of research questions that I have pursued as a scientist. The scientific training I received in graduate school provided me the tools I utilize daily in designing experiments, executing projects, and interpreting data. But ultimately, the tools that my parents and family have given me—a sense of compassion for others, dedication, and a commitment to learning—have been equally important in rounding out my life experiences and helping me to keep things in perspective. Finally, I am truly blessed with a life partner who understands the passion and commitment I have for science and research—a commitment that drives me to work long hours in the lab and takes me to faraway places.

Finally, in the spirit of Robert Frost's poem, two roads diverged in the woods, one for the M.D. and the other for the Ph.D. I took both paths, and that has made all the difference.

Acknowledgments:

As always, I attribute whatever success I have had to a divine source, and accept all of my failings as that of my own doing.

Questions to ask yourself before you join a lab:

What type of person are you?
independent
team player
need nurturing
need high pressure/stress
need stature/prominence

Does your lab choice draw upon/enhance your personality type?

What components do you need for optimal performance?
make your own schedule
receive high or low supervision
have access to resources

Is it a teaching environment?
You should find out if there are postdoctoral fellows, graduate students, or technicians who are familiar with techniques you might be using. Find out if the people in the lab are willing to teach you new techniques that you are not familiar with.

Does the culture fit your personality?
Some labs have people who work from 9 a.m. to 5 p.m. and others have people who work all night. Every lab has its own culture, from the type of music people play to the kind of hours people work. Find out if your personality fits the lab culture.

Questions to ask yourself while you are choosing a research project:

Do you want to create or extend?

Will you be working on a project that you will develop and create from scratch, or will you be working on extensions of the work of other people who have left or are currently in the lab? For certain personalities, one option might be more appealing than the other.

Do you want a high-, medium-, or low-risk project?

Some people choose a first project that has an interesting outcome regardless of whether it involves negative or positive data. This approach allows publishable results no matter what the outcomes are. Others choose a project that has a higher risk, thus giving them a better chance—if it works—to publish in a top-tier journal. As you choose your research project, think ahead.

CHAPTER 8

What to Expect as a Practicing Physician in Today's Complex Medical Environment

By Malik White, M.D.

Why Medicine? My Path and Current Experience

For many of you who will read this book, perhaps my story begins in a similar fashion to yours. My formative years were spent in a lower-middle class neighborhood in a small city in Northern California. During my sophomore year in high school, I watched a film that explored possible career choices. At that time, I had a very basic understanding of medicine. I was interested in studying biology, I had a basic desire to help people, and I enjoyed working with children. Being a pediatrician seemed like a good fit. I was fortunate to have parents who instilled in me a pride and understanding of the history of African-Americans in this country. I was keenly aware of the need for physicians and role models in the black community. By the beginning of college, my goal was clear and basic: I wanted to be a physician so that I could take care of sick children and be a role model in my community.

I attended a local college, San Jose State University, where I earned a bachelor of science degree in the biological sciences. Having always been fascinated by large metropolitan areas, I went to New York City for medical school at Cornell University Medical College. I experienced an incredible four-year journey through the Big Apple, and I earned a doctor of medicine degree. After medical school, I returned home to Northern California to complete my internship and residency training (three years) in general pediatrics at the University of California, San Francisco. (Residency training occurs after medical school. It is the process of learning how to become a practicing physician in a specific field of medicine—surgery, adult medicine, psychiatry, etc. The first year of residency training is called internship, or the intern year, and these first-year doctors are known as interns.)

After seven years of intense study and on-the-job training—four years of medical school and three years of internship/residency—I was ready to enter the world of modern medicine as an attending physician. (An attending/supervising physician is a doctor who has finished residency training and is fully responsible for the patient and the medical team.) I chose to become an independent contractor/per diem physician immediately after I finished training. My arrangement is simple. I work shifts (twelve, sixteen or twenty-four hours long) at different hospitals, providing care only for pediatric patients. I work fourteen to seventeen shifts each month; I am off the other fourteen to fifteen days. I have complete control of my schedule, which is made one to three months in advance.

I have worked simultaneously at many hospitals (up to fourteen) and have treated patients in all areas of pediatric medicine: the emergency room, the neonatal (infant) and pediatric intensive care units, the hospital floor, and the general clinic. Working in three major metropolitan areas—the San Francisco Bay Area, Los Angeles, and New York City—I have provided care in almost every type of hospital environment. These include public county/ municipal hospitals, university teaching centers, private not-for-profit hospitals, and health maintenance organizations. I have cared for patients from numerous ethnic backgrounds and all rungs of the socioeconomic ladder. My experience as an attending physician during the past six years has afforded me a special view through a unique window into modern American medicine. I hope to share with you my insight into being a doctor in today's complex medical environment.

The Hospital Environment and the Training Process

For all intern and resident physicians and for those of us attending physicians who choose to work in the hospital, the day is typically long and fast. It starts as you receive a report from the overnight physician about the status of your patients. Typically, you will be responsible for six to ten patients as an intern and up to twenty to thirty patients as a senior resident or attending doctor. Throughout the morning, the medical team—which consists of the attending physician, resident and intern physicians, medical students, and often a pharmacist—will make work rounds on each patient. During this time, the patient's disease, examination findings, lab results, medications, and therapeutic plans will be thoroughly discussed among all members of the team. In addition, this time is used to teach members about specific aspects of a given disease process. The attending physician is responsible for directing the overall flow of work rounds, which typically last three to five hours.

After work rounds, the real work of the day has to be done. The paperwork has to be completed; patient progress notes have to be written, and lab results have to be obtained and documented. The patients who need to be discharged from the hospital have numerous forms—prescriptions, follow-up appointments, and home health visits—that have to be finalized. There are many meetings with specialist physicians. During X-ray rounds, radiologist physicians will explain X-rays and other imaging studies (CT scan, MRI, sonogram, etc.). Some patients may require the services of a heart, kidney, blood, or gastrointestinal specialist. Each of these specialist physicians will meet with the team throughout the day, and his or her recommendations have to be implemented.

More meetings occur with social workers and discharge planners concerning the home situation and well-being of your patients once they leave the hospital. For patients with more complicated conditions, there may be family meetings with translators and social workers to explain the specifics of a long hospital stay. Several teaching conferences exist throughout the week where attending physicians, residents and interns, and medical students will each present patient cases and stimulate interactive discussions.

"Beep, beep, beep." The pager goes off again. "This is Dr. White, pediatrics." The doctor on the other end of the phone says, "There is a four-year-old child with asthma and a right lower lobe pneumonia here in the emergency room. We have given her three albuterol nebs, one atrovent neb, and a dose of Ceftriaxone. The patient is still having some difficulty breathing and is on five liters of face-mask oxygen. Could you please come and see her?" Amid all the chaos of the day, there are still more sick patients who need your services. The child in the emergency room has to be seen in an expedient manner, evaluated, and brought to the hospital floor with specific orders indicating her treatment plan. There can be as many as five to ten admissions to the floor and at times an equal number of discharges every day. The pace is well beyond hectic. Your day will eventually end nine to twelve hours after it started as you give a report on your patients to the overnight physician.

The nighttime hospital culture is a different monster. During the training years, every intern and resident physician will inevitably spend many nights in the hospital caring for patients until the sun rises. Some attending physicians (particularly those of us who work in the emergency room or intensive care unit) enjoy the night culture. We call it "adrenaline medicine," a time when we get to focus on treating many extremely ill patients. There are no executives or administrators, social workers, or discharge planners in the hospital at that time. Fewer doctors, nurses, support staff, and services are available overnight. Each physician—attending or resident/intern—has much more responsibility in making patient-care decisions, as there are far fewer people around to provide input or advice. Basically, the night shift boils down to this: no meetings or conferences, minimal red tape, and many sick patients to treat.

If you are a high school or premedical college student, you probably can't imagine the seriousness and incredibly rapid pace of a large hospital. When I first started volunteering in the emergency room as a college student, I would be equally terrified and fascinated by an extremely sick patient brought in by ambulance. I would watch in amazement as the doctors treated and stabilized the patient, and I would think to myself, "Am I going to be able to do this?" Early on in medical school, after learning how to do a basic examination, I would wonder, "How am I ever going to be able to take care of a whole floor of sick patients?"

What happens is that you are tutored through the process, step by step, by scientists and physicians who have twenty to thirty years of experience in their respective fields of study. First, you read many books and attend many lectures. Next, your hand is held as you examine your first patient. You continue to read and prepare as you make your first patient presentation to a group of attending physicians. Somewhere along the way, you learn how to work faster and more efficiently to keep up with the hectic pace as you are slowly given more patient-care responsibilities. You get to make one or two decisions under direct supervision. Finally, you are allowed to make medical decisions on you own. You are now free to venture off into the world to practice the art of medicine. It is, at a minimum, a seven-year process of fifty to a hundred hours per week devoted to learning about disease and healing.

After Residency Training:
Working as a Physician in Today's Medical Environment

The training period is finished; now, how are you going to generate income and get paid? There are three basic options: (1) work for an employer; (2) open or join a private practice; or (3) contract your services as an independent provider. Most physicians work for an employer (as a staff doctor) when they have completed training.

The different employers include private or public hospitals, health maintenance organizations, academic/university teaching centers, or clinic foundations. The majority of the full-time staff doctors will work an average of forty to sixty hours a week, with two to three weekends off each month. As a staff doctor you are guaranteed salary, vacation, malpractice and health insurance, and pension benefits. Weekend and overnight patient coverage, also known as "on-call" coverage, is split among a large group of physicians; this means you may only have to work on-call two to three extra nights and perhaps one weekend each month.

Another option is to join an existing private practice or start one on your own. There is a significant amount of extra work involved with running a business—including paying administrative salaries, billing for services, purchasing equipment, and leasing office space—in addition to the stresses of practicing medicine. The size of the group of doctors in the practice can have an effect on how much on-call coverage you have to provide. If there are three physicians in the group practice, then every third night you will be responsible for addressing the medical needs of your practice's patients. The weekly workload can range from fifty to ninety hours, depending on the on-call coverage arrangement. The benefit of private practice lies within the financial reward. There is great potential for making a significantly higher salary compared with those staff doctors who work for employers. Also, after many years of building the practice, the schedule can become more flexible with increased leisure time and less on-call coverage.

The primary benefit of working as an independent contractor is having complete control of your schedule. You only work the shifts for which you contract; there is no on-call coverage. Typically, there is much less paperwork and fewer meetings, as the contractor is not a member of the hospital staff. However, the salary is not guaranteed. If you become ill and cannot work, you don't receive a paycheck. There are no health insurance or retirement benefits; these things have to be paid for by the contractor. Malpractice insurance, which can be extremely costly, may be an expense that you have to cover.

Now that you have determined how the money is being deposited into your bank account, in what setting are you going to care for patients? Most patients do not require hospitalization; rather, they visit their physicians in the outpatient setting—the clinic or office. It follows that the vast majority of doctors spend most of their time caring for patients in a clinic or office setting. The typical outpatient workday is from 8 a.m. to 6 p.m. with a small break for lunch. A smaller percentage of physicians (less than 25 percent) work solely in the hospital, also known as the inpatient setting. Averaging between fifty and eighty hours, the inpatient workweek is typically longer than the clinic or office workweek. Many physicians split their time between inpatient and outpatient settings, with the percent of time spent in each arena determined by personal preference and the particular medical field or specialty.

Do all doctors participate in hands-on patient care? For many physicians the answer, surprisingly, is no. One of my colleagues now works in hospital administration. Formulating treatment strategies for specific diseases, distributing funds and resources to different departments in the hospital, and creating health and wellness plans for the hospital community are some of the daily issues that a physician administrator tackles. Another colleague creates and coordinates major research efforts and drug distribution projects for the treatment of AIDS in Africa. Devising health policy strategy (plans to prevent and treat diseases affecting entire communities) at the city, state, and federal level is another avenue of employment for doctors. Some physicians work for pharmaceutical companies, where they control large drug research budgets and direct the distribution of new drugs to patients and hospitals. As you can see, there are many roles that doctors need to fill, many of which involve little or no patient care.

Throughout college, medical school, and residency, I thought that doctors worked in the hospital or office every day, putting in long hours taking care of patients week in and week out. But while the vast majority of doctors provide care to patients, many of us also work in the administrative, research, and business branches of medicine. I have also noticed that more and more physicians are taking control of their time. Colleagues have opted to work a half or three-quarter time staff position (with a proportional reduction in pay) in order to spend more time with family. In an attempt to increase flexibility in their schedule, many doctors choose to work for more than one employer or work part time as an employee and part time as an independent contractor. I now see that there are many options for the work setting and daily routine of doctors. Furthermore, there are many avenues in this vast field of medicine for current and future physicians to explore.

The Challenges of Modern Medicine

The costs of a medical education continue to rise. This concern weighs heavily on the minds of most premedical students and in some cases may deter potential physicians from choosing this career path. Medical education debt can exceed $70,000 in a public (state) medical school and can total more than $180,000 at some private institutions. Most medical students take out student loans to cover these costs. The average debt of an American medical school graduate in 2002 was greater than $100,000.

It would be foolish to say that the cost of a medical education should not be a concern. You are fully responsible for paying back a large sum of money—in some cases enough to have purchased a home. However, the costs of the education should *not* be a major factor in your decision about whether to pursue a medical degree. When you are finally working as an attending physician, your salary will be more than enough to cover the repayment costs. I do not have any colleagues who cannot afford their monthly loan payments. Although my medical school loans totaled more than $130,000, repayment has not been a major issue. Furthermore, I am glad that the increased cost of a private education did not deter me from choosing to attend Cornell University Medical College.

The greatest challenge by far is maintaining the dedication and effort needed to accomplish the tasks at hand: medical school and internship/residency training. Most premedical college students, and probably the majority of first-year medical students, don't understand the horrors of internship and residency training. You work extremely hard in medical school. Simply put, you have to work harder during the training years. You are no longer considered a medical student. By this time, you have earned a doctor of medicine degree and are expected to take care of a large number of patients. The hours are long, and mental and physical exhaustion is commonplace. You are under a microscope the entire time, critiqued at every step. You endure constant scrutiny as you are guided through the process of becoming a practicing physician.

In the third month of my internship, I sat crouched in a hospital corridor at four in the morning. I was twenty-two hours into a thirty-hour day—with eight hours to go. I was looking at vital signs of several unstable patients, and I was absolutely exhausted. "I don't know if I can do this every fourth night for the next three years," I said to myself. I tucked my head between my knees in a moment of temporary defeat. The comforting hand of one of my co-interns touched my shoulder. "Yeah, this is horrible," she said. "But we chose to do this. And it will be over soon enough." Her simple words resonated in my psyche for the rest of my training. I did *choose* to do this. And the reason I chose to do this is because I had a goal to one day take care of sick children. My unwavering commitment to achieving that goal was the driving force that allowed me to endure the exhaustion and ills of the training period.

Beyond the training years, many other challenges exist. Medical malpractice lawsuits have increased dramatically over the past two decades and continue to be a source of fear. This fear has slowly changed the way doctors practice medicine. Physicians now use the "defensive medicine" approach, where excessive laboratory and radiology tests (X-rays, CT scans, sonograms, etc.) are ordered so that the physician is covered in the event of a malpractice lawsuit. This method of practice ultimately leads to a waste of resources, the exposure of patients to unnecessary risks (i.e., X-ray radiation) without significant benefit, and patient expectations that more tests should be done to treat their illness, which creates a vicious cycle. This approach to treating patients is not healthy for medicine on the whole. However, "defensive medicine" is utilized to some extent by almost all practicing physicians given the reality of our society's propensity for seeking litigation against doctors.

The Internet has also created new challenges for physicians. Now armed with a wealth of information (not all of which is accurate), educated patients come to the doctor's office with their own treatment plans in mind. Because there is much more access to medical data and advice today, these well-read patients are more likely to question the physician's plans and judgment. In some cases, the patient or parent may know more than the doctor does about a certain rare disease that a family member or child has. Other times, patients may request newly emerging treatment options that have not been fully studied and may not be covered by their insurance policies. In this new information era, physicians often find themselves negotiating between what they believe is the right treatment approach based on their experience with treating disease and what the patients believes is the right thing to do based on the massive amount of literature available to them online.

As an African-American physician, there is the added task of contributing back to my community, which is starving for positive role models. There is often pressure for young medical students of color to choose careers as general practitioners (adult medicine, pediatrics, family practice) so that they can return to their respective communities to practice general medicine. While physicians of color are desperately needed to provide medical care in minority communities, one does not have to practice in a poor, minority community to contribute. Underrepresented minority physicians need to pursue and advance in all areas of medicine; other areas include surgical subspecialties (cardiothoracic surgery, plastic surgery, neurosurgery, etc.), research, academics, and administration. There are many ways to contribute outside of direct patient care, such as volunteering with community or church groups, participating in forums, and mentoring students, to name a few. By working with other young underrepresented minority doctors and scientists who are themselves committed to community involvement, it is becoming easier for me to integrate the role model aspect into my responsibilities as a practicing physician.

Finally, one of the most serious issues a physician faces is talking to patients and families about suffering and death. The goal of medicine is to prevent or treat disease in the human body; however, illness oftentimes overwhelms the body, and life passes away. During the training process, all physicians will come face to face with death and will have to speak to family members about the passing of a loved one. Doctors must attempt to understand their own thoughts as well as try to incorporate the family's views and cultural approach to this sensitive subject. A physician often takes on the role of counselor during times of despair. In a position that may be neither familiar nor comfortable, doctors often play a key supportive role during what can be the worst of times for the family of a dying patient.

I was working a quiet Sunday afternoon shift in a large New York City emergency room. The call came in overhead: "Sixteen-year-old collapsed at the airport. Intubated in the field (breathing tube placed into the windpipe). CPR ongoing. Estimated time of arrival—two minutes." Immediately, I had an ominous feeling. Teenagers are generally healthy. Sixteen-year-olds don't just collapse and need cardiopulmonary resuscitation. The ambulance arrived, and a teenage female was wheeled into the ER. "Almost fifteen minutes of CPR, atropine and epinephrine given times two, still no pulse," the paramedic blurted. I quickly attempted to intervene. A rapid blood gas analysis confirmed that her heart had probably stopped pumping blood to her body; there was far too much acid in her system for any hope of a recovery. I called the code and pronounced her dead.

Next came one of the worst moments in my entire career as a physician. The social worker had led the family into a quiet room so that I could speak with them. As I entered the room, the anxious and desperate eyes of a mother and sister were fixed upon me. I then had to explain to them that a healthy, vibrant sixteen-year-old who was getting ready to go on her first flight to visit relatives in California had just passed away from an apparent heart attack. There is no way to describe the sadness and grief that engulfed the room at that time. I have had to speak to family members about the death of a child several times. The unease lessens slightly with each experience, but it is by far the most difficult duty I have to perform as a physician.

The Rewards of Practicing Medicine

I'm sure many of you are interested in the financial compensation for all of the years of hard work. I always tell high school and college students who are interested in becoming a doctor: Do not go into medicine for the money. You can get an M.B.A. (master's in business administration) or a J.D. (juris doctor—law degree) and potentially make far more money in half the time it takes to complete medical school and residency training. I truly believe that medicine is a calling. Some innate desire to heal must exist—and that desire will propel you through the immense hardships and allow you to make the sacrifices necessary to become a practicing physician. If you do choose to undertake this rigorous course, the financial rewards are plentiful.

In terms of wages, physicians are compensated based on the number of years of medical training *after* the completion of medical school. General internal (adult) medicine, general pediatrics, and family practice all require three years of training. These physicians make $100,000 to $120,000 per year as new attendings. Most adult medicine and pediatric subspecialists (heart, intensive care unit, cancer, etc.) train for another three years (six total years of training) and can expect to make $30,000 to $50,000 more than their general physician counterparts. Emergency room physicians train for three or four years, and their earnings start at $150,000 to $170,000 per year.

In general, doctors who operate tend to make more money, because the cost of performing a surgery is substantial. General obstetrics/gynecology (delivering babies and operating on the female reproductive system) requires four to five years of training; their salaries start near $200,000 per year. Surgical subspecialists (bone, kidney transplant, heart, etc.) typically train for six to ten years and start in the $200,000 range. By the time most of you reading this book begin practicing medicine, the salaries listed above will have changed based on the country's demand for the services of the particular specialty. However, the key point is that as a physician, you will make enough money to enjoy a very comfortable lifestyle and to provide more than adequately for your family.

From my current perspective, the money is secondary to the pleasure I derive from practicing medicine. There is immense satisfaction gained from touching an individual's life through the power of healing. I find it extremely gratifying when I am able to diagnose a disease process in a critically ill child, intervene with a particular medication or procedure, and follow the child as he or she fights the illness and eventually walks (or runs) out of the hospital. Through direct intervention, such as when plastic tubes are threaded through the umbilical cord into an infant's heart, and through choosing medications and treatment strategies, caring for an ill patient is a constant intellectual and physical challenge that never becomes routine.

The rewards continue with the thanks and praise received from patients and family members. Most individuals realize the incredible sacrifice one makes to become a physician. People are generally very grateful for your concern and help when you are treating their loved one. Although you often wonder, "why am I doing this?" during the rigorous training years, you are constantly reminded of the worth of this profession by the appreciation that is expressed to you on a regular basis.

Since the beginning of modern civilization, medicine and its practitioners have been a major pillar of every community. Even in this complex, technology-driven era, physicians are still valued for their achievements and contributions. Despite the staggering number of medical malpractice lawsuits and the significant amount of consumer discontent with medical care, physicians are still held in high esteem in the eyes of the general public. Many sectors of society, including church associations, student and elderly groups, small businesses, and corporations, will regularly call on you to share your knowledge and motivate others. Friends, family, neighbors, and the community at large all grant me a certain respect for this calling that I have chosen to undertake and for the dedication that I have displayed in pursuing this field of study.

The Goal Achieved and Beyond

I am now moving forward in my career to new heights that I never knew were possible. As of July 2004, I returned to the training process as a fellow (a physician who has already finished a residency training program to undertake further medical training in a particular subspecialty) in intensive care unit medicine for children at the University of California, Los Angeles.

My plans are to train in the fellowship for three years and then to work for five to ten years as a clinical professor of pediatrics at a major academic medical center. As a professor, my responsibilities will include teaching medical students and intern/resident physicians and caring for ill children in the intensive care unit setting. I will continue to develop and eventually implement a health professions recruitment and mentoring program for high school, college, and medical school students from African-American and underrepresented Latino backgrounds. Although practicing medicine in the modern era has many complexities, in a way it is very simple. What I do now is exactly what I had initially set out to do—take care of sick children and be a role model in my community.

CHAPTER 9

Trust Me… I'm a Doctor: Advice/Tips on How to Maximize Your Potential in College and Medical School

By Brandee L. Waite, M.D.

"Trust me… I'm a doctor." These words were boldly printed on a T-shirt worn by a healthy-looking middle-aged man I met at a gym. He was doing the chest press machine, and as he opened his arm to return the machine to the starting position, "Trust me…" called out from the front of his shirt. As he stood from the reclined seat, "…I'm a doctor," answered on the back. When I inquired, he laughed and said his wife got the shirt for him as a joke because it seemed that everyone he met, after finding out he was a physician, would ask him what to do about some problem they had. At the time, I was applying to medical school and had no idea how I would come to appreciate the humor of that shirt. Now, having been a physician for nearly five years, I'm always amazed that complete strangers will seek my opinion about some personal issue (usually providing way more intimate information than I ever wanted to hear) just because they overhear me mention my profession. I always oblige, and people genuinely seem to appreciate my advice, though I'm never quite sure why. I could be a raving lunatic with a doctor complex and they would never know the difference. When I was approached about writing a chapter for this book, I initially had the same feeling. Why would complete strangers listen to what I have to say about gaining one's competitive edge in medicine and science? In this instance, however, I can provide some proof of my qualifications for commentary. I did not come from wealth, none of my family members had careers in medicine or science, I am a woman of color, and I have been accused of being a social butterfly on more than one occasion (read: I am not a bookworm). Not quite the lineage you'd expect for a physician whose resume boasts an undergraduate degree (with honors) from Stanford University, a medical doctorate from University of California, San Francisco, a Stanford Medical Center residency, and a Johns Hopkins University Hospital fellowship. Needless to say, in order to achieve this educational pedigree, I have relied heavily on two things: the grace of God and my ability to succeed despite formidable competition. In this chapter, I'll share with you a list of tips that are quite useful for navigating college and medical school and performing at the top of your game. This is what worked for me. Trust me... I'm a doctor.

Tips to Maximize Your Potential in College

1. Visit colleges before you choose which you'll attend.

   Go and check out as many campuses as you can afford to before you make a decision about where to go. At least try to visit your top three choices once you've been accepted. Many schools have some type of pre-admit weekend during spring semester where they arrange special activities for potential incoming students. Ask if this type of activity is available. It is a fantastic opportunity to see what it really feels like to be at that college. You'll get to meet other students and ask them questions about what classes are like, what the options are for the social scene, and whether they are getting the education they want. You'll be able to see firsthand what the dorms are like—this is no small point. Some schools require freshmen to live on campus, so seeing what the housing options are in person could affect your decision. My freshman dorm room had bunk beds, and a half-sized closet that I shared with my randomly assigned roommate. I knew all of this ahead of time, so it was no big deal. Some of those who hadn't been able to visit were quite surprised with their living quarters and had a bit of an adjustment period. You'll also get a chance to preview some of the clubs, study resources, and activities that are available to students. This exposure helps to alleviate some of the anxiety about starting at a new place, and allows you to feel comfortable that you have chosen the institution that is best for you.

2. Join at least one academic and one non-academic student group.

Most academic student groups are extracurricular associations of students with common academic goals (Premed Association, National Society of Black Scientists and Engineers, Women in Science, etc). They have resources that are quite helpful. They allow you access to older students who will have great advice on scheduling classes, which professors are better, how to best study for specific tests, among other things. They can also provide you with old notes and used books. Be careful not to join too many groups early on, however, or you'll be overwhelmed.

Non-academic groups are for fun. They give you something to look forward to and help decrease stress. You'll be exposed to people in other majors for more friendship and networking opportunities. Medical schools do look for well-rounded candidates, so this is for your own sanity *and* your resume. I joined a sorority and a dance company. The sorority actually provided me with community service and volunteer activities that were rewarding and helped beef up my resume. The dance company helped me relieve stress, stay in shape, and maintain participation in an activity in which I excelled and enjoyed myself even when I felt I was struggling with academics.

3. Choose courses wisely.

Seek advice from older students/upperclassmen in your major regarding issues such as which semester and what order is best for taking certain classes. These things can affect your grades. Don't be afraid to design your own course of study within your major if allowed, or even to design your own major. You'll get a better GPA if you actually like your coursework. You may discover other aspects or branches of your field that you enjoy, and this will give an opportunity to explore them.

Also consider taking premed prerequisites at another school if your university allows it. This can be done over the summers at junior colleges or smaller universities. I think this was one of the keys in maximizing my GPA. I took physics and organic chemistry over the summers and did very well in these and other courses that were more difficult for me. The classes are usually smaller, so it's easier to get help. The grades transfer into your GPA just as if you had taken them during the regular year. During summer session you usually take only one class, so there are no conflicting academic requirements to tear you away from focused study. The classes are accelerated, though, so you can get into trouble if you fall behind. Also, taking classes over the summer allows you to take fewer units during the year and still be on track for graduation.

4. Go to at least one "big game."

There is nothing like the roar of the crowd at a "big game" with the stands packed full of team colors. Will it directly help you get into medical school? No. But participating in a rite of traditional rivalry like this will give you school ties and foster pride in being part of a thriving student body and alumni group. The feeling of loyalty and fun that predominates at these events is fantastic. In fact, I have been to every Stanford football "big game" since my freshman year in college. Fourteen in a row—didn't miss one during med school, or even internship or residency, because they are just that fun. Experiencing this type of school pride/spirit indirectly motivated me at times, because I always wanted to be a shining representative of my university. Basketball and football generally have the biggest fan base, so whether or not you are truly a sports fan, you will enjoy being caught up in the excitement of the event. Do not make the mistake of discounting the value of this common mainstream college experience in promoting personal well-being. Trust me...

Tips Applicable to College and Medical School

1. Party as a break from studies—don't study as a break from parties.

    College is the first time most people will be living without constant parental input. Don't lose your mind! I grew up in a fairly strict household, so I was raring to go when I moved onto campus, but I knew I could not let my new social freedoms jeopardize my pursuit of medical school. There will be *lots* of parties; missing one will not ruin your college experience. On the flip side, you do need to go out and enjoy yourself in an unstructured manner at least once in a while, just to relax. Parties are a treat every college student has earned and should be able to enjoy. A general rule is to party on Friday or Saturday night—not both on a regular basis. It is a way to cut loose with other students/friends, and you need that release in order to prevent burnout. You will have a lot of work. Especially in medical school, it is impossible to do all the reading, no matter how hard you try. If drunken debauchery at the frat house or local bar is not your scene, check out dance parties or musical performances, or just go to the movies and out for burgers with a group of friends. Just remember that there will always be another party but your exams are a one-time shot, so plan accordingly.

2. Use study groups, but not exclusively.

Group study is more important in college and medical school than it is in high school. Other people have different strengths, insights, and perceptions that can help you understand material better. Also, explaining what you know to others will help you truly get a grasp on what you think you know. I was more likely to join study groups for classes that I found more difficult in college and for nearly everything in med school. I can recall specific items that I learned in a study group but hadn't understood in regular lecture that later showed up on tests. Reviewing the material ahead of time helps to identify areas where you are weak, so you'll know what questions to ask at study sessions. Reviewing it after the group lets you follow up and solidify what you just learned or just realized you needed to learn. You don't have to study with friends. In fact, choosing a study group based on your section leader in college or combining different sections in medical school will enhance your fund of knowledge while decreasing time spent in idle chatter.

3. Take care of your health.

Everyone hears about the "freshman fifteen" within the first week of starting college. This term refers to the fifteen pounds that most students gain during freshman year. Dorm food, alcohol, decreased physical activity—these all can contribute to a decline in overall health and energy. You've got to take care of your health in order to be at your best mentally and academically. Participate in some type of exercise or sporting activity at least once a week. Go to the student health center for regular checkups. It is much easier to keep up with your health needs during college and med school than it is during residency, so take advantage.

Be aware of your use of drugs and/or alcohol. Again, you'll be living on your own and making choices without immediate parental intervention, so living fast and loose can be enticing. There is no denying that you will encounter some intelligent people who use drugs. They are smart *despite* their drug use, not because of it, and eventually it can catch up with them. In addition, you'll also notice that drugs and alcohol are by no means a requirement on the party scene. Plenty of cool people party sober and have a blast. Make your choices wisely, because there are some jobs (summer and long-term internships/work positions) that do require drug testing.

Lastly, use condoms every time you have sex! Most people in college and med school are having sex, and if you choose to join their ranks, do so responsibly. We all are aware of the HIV risk and consequences. This is a life-and-death issue. Even on a lesser scale, other curable STDs can be uncomfortable and embarrassing, and it is a hassle to make extra clinic trips for treatment of a completely preventable infection. An unplanned pregnancy can change your life if you and your partner choose to have/keep the baby, or can cause undue stress and worry if you decide not to have the baby. I have to use more than one hand to count the number of friends who had the stress of an unwanted pregnancy affect their educational experience. Be safe, so you can be unhampered in your pursuit of academic goals—it's hard enough without added, avoidable stressors.

4. Have a plan for when things get tough.

No matter how smart you are, there will be tough academic times. I can distinctly recall heaving a textbook across the room in frustration and wanting to rip out every freaking page, screaming "I hate this! I hate it, I hate it!" I knew people who got mired down in this frustration and could not bounce back. Your ability to recover from these setbacks will set you apart. Know what, who, and where your supports are so you can get help when you need it. Talk to family; they will remind you how wonderful you are and how proud they are of you. Commiserate with other students, because sometimes just venting makes you feel better. Also talk to friends who are on different paths (i.e. working, starting families, or otherwise not in school) to regain some perspective on why you're doing what you're doing. Go to church/temple/spiritual/religious gatherings to help renew your faith in the positive forces guiding the universe and watching over you. Everyone will face hard times personally, academically, or financially during the educational journey. Finding a timely, healthy way through these difficulties will serve you well. An hour or two of prevention in this realm can be worth days or weeks of cure, so don't wait for things to fall apart completely before using your support network.

5. Do research projects and volunteer work for experience, resume-building, and letters of recommendation.

You need some volunteer work or community service activities on your resume. You also need letters of recommendation to get into college, medical school, and residency. You can never have too many reference letters, so request them from anyone who witnesses your successes, especially in any science-related courses/projects. Ask professors and project leaders for letters immediately as you finish their course/project. A letter written with fresh experience in mind will be far better than one written one or two years after you've completed the work. Allow plenty of time for writers to meet deadlines (at least four, if not six, weeks). It sounds redundant, but be sure to ask if they feel they can write a positive letter for you. I did not do this with my letters of recommendation for medical school, and the consequences were almost life-altering.

I had a letter for med school written by an academic adviser who was less than favorable in her opinion of me and my work. I was shocked to walk into an interview and be asked, "What was the problem in your work with _____?" I had received grades of A- and B+ in difficult courses from the writer, and I could not believe the negative things that were written about me in that letter. (One interviewer was kind enough to read it to me so I could know what to prepare as a rebuttal for future interviews.) Not long after, the writer was diagnosed with an uncommon neurological condition that affected judgment and thought process. But it would have been too late for me—I could have potentially not gotten into medical school because of this letter. Luckily, it was in such contrast to the other letters in my file that every interviewer gave me the benefit of the doubt in my explanations. Don't take that chance with your future—just ask for a positive letter at the outset and you'll be fine.

6. You are not a loser if you take time off, change majors, or decide medicine is not for you!

   Over half of the students who start out in premed change to another course of study during college. During my sophomore year in college, I lived in a suite with five roommates. Five of us started out in premed; four decided to go to med school; three graduated from med school, and all of us took time off for research or a planned "break." Some former premeds decide to pursue the basic sciences; others move toward public health fields. There are many fantastic careers in health and science that are not as well known as traditional medicine, and it can take time to discover these other pathways. Some former premeds leave health/science completely. There are people who leave medical school as well. It does not mean that they are weak or less intelligent. Medicine is a wonderful field, but it is hard work, for long hours, and for long years, with delayed financial gratification. It is not worth struggling through and missing out on the things you will have to miss unless you really love it. Trust me...

Tips to Maximize Your Potential in Medical School

1. Apply to and interview at all the schools you can.

   Medical school applicant pools become more and more competitive each year. Apply to as many schools as you can to increase your odds and possibly provide yourself with choices. Do not limit your applications to one tier—try for at least a few top-ranked schools. Most of your applications will go to average-level schools, and I don't believe there is such a thing as a "safety" school when it comes to medicine, because they are all hard to get into. Different schools are looking for different qualities in their students, so don't be discouraged if you are not offered an interview at a particular place. Case in point: I was accepted at the University of California, San Francisco, which was consistently ranked by *U.S. News and World Report* as a medical school in of the top five in the nation, yet I was not even invited to interview at some other non-ranking schools. When applying to residency, you will interview with several programs and then submit a "match list" in which you rank the programs in the order you wish to attend (first choice, second choice, etc.). When filing the final draft of your match list, be sure to rank every program at which you interviewed. You should only omit programs that you definitely would not attend. Don't believe any program director who says, "Only rank us, because we'll choose you for sure." Programs close and people transfer and, unless you've listed every acceptable alternative choice, you could end up not matching into a residency program.

2. Be confident in interviews.

    You've worked hard and have good grades and letters, so be proud of your accomplishments and confident when presenting yourself in interviews. Self-questioning or deprecating remarks will not make you seem humble; they'll make you seem insecure. Cockiness should also be avoided. Dress professionally, not frumpy or flashy. Style and class don't hurt—looking good will never count against you.

People told me not to wear pants because some interviewers are old-fashioned and prefer women to wear skirt suits. I did not find that to be true at all. Honestly, I was complimented on my suits (pants and skirts) on 25 to 50 percent of my interviews. It sounds trite, but just be yourself—and be confident. Having a personality makes you memorable. I recall one interview that took place in a faculty member's office on the top floor of a tall building on a hill overlooking the city. The view was breathtaking, and I commented on it as soon as I had introduced myself. The interviewer smiled and stated, "The view is the reason I chose this office. I have been interviewing applicants in here for years and you are the first one to notice the view. I can tell you'll see the big picture and be a good doctor." Needless to say, that interview went quite well because the tone was set early with a comment that showed just a bit of my personality.

3. Be open-minded when doing your clerkships.

The third and fourth years of med school consist of rotations/clerkships in different specialties. It's fine to have an idea of what you want to go into, but don't dismiss other possibilities. Prior to rotations, most students have an idea of what it means to be an orthopedic surgeon, an internist, a pediatrician, or a gynecologist. What they likely do not know what it means to be a rheumatologist, a radiation oncologist, a physiatrist, or an endocrinologist. I ended up in a field of medicine I never even heard of until my third year of medical school. Remember, *you* are the one who has to get up and go to work year in and year out, so choose the field that you enjoy the most.

Don't put too much stock in perceived prestige or money or what fields "people like you" usually go into. Just because you're a woman doesn't mean you have to do ob/gyn, pediatrics, or family practice. Just because you're an athlete doesn't mean you have to do orthopedic surgery or ER. All of these possibilities are available, but your preferred lifestyle and family commitments should be considered. It will be very difficult for female physicians to have multiple children during residency, but not impossible. Maintaining a long-distance relationship, caring for an elderly parent, or continuing your fun weekend job as a bartender would be hard to do as a surgery resident, but it has been done.

A final word of advice on clerkships: psychiatry helps with everything, because crazy people have all kinds of medical problems that you'll have to treat. So pay attention on this rotation even if you don't think you'll ever use it, because I guarantee you will. Trust me...

One-Liners to Remember

You will suck at something.

Don't date your professors or attending physicians.

Do date people outside of medicine and science.

Have Fun Along the Way

Having fun along the way is the one thing about which I'm most passionate. The process of becoming a physician takes at least eleven years, and likely more (counting college, medical school, and residency), depending on your path. You will be a happier person, and thus a better doctor, if you nurture your body, spirit, personal life, and sense of humor as you go. The things you do to keep your sanity can be as rewarding and influential as the educational process itself. Allow me one last personal example to tie it all together.

I grew up watching football with my dad. He swears my first words were, "Touchdown, Forty-Niners!" I decided I wanted to be a doctor before kindergarten, and started saying I was going to deliver babies by fifth grade. In high school I was a dancer, varsity athlete, honors student, and cheerleader. In college, I joined a dance company; worked in the department of athletics; majored in human biology, concentrating on women's health and fitness; and took physics in summer school after my freshman and sophomore years. During junior year I took a one-unit PE course to learn how to be an aerobics instructor and then taught fitness classes as a break from studies the following summer. Senior year I started dating a football player and decided to take a year off after graduating before starting medical school. One of my summer aerobics jobs was affiliated with a luxury health spa in Mexico, and I was offered a one-year position teaching fitness classes and living at the spa and on an international cruise ship. I took that job and had the time of my life while I was applying to medical school.

I started medical school fully intent on becoming an obstetrician/gynecologist, continued taking occasional dance classes, kept dating the football player, and taught two fitness classes a week to make extra money. After taking Step 1 of the U.S. Medical License Examination (USMLE) at the end of my second year, my boyfriend went into the NFL and I went on vacation with a group of med student friends. One was reading a book on careers in medicine and began to read out loud about the field of physical medicine and rehabilitation (physiatry) because she thought it sounded like something I'd do. I had never heard of it and didn't believe that it was even a real specialty. I decided to do an elective rotation in physiatry, which is much like neurologic and orthopedic rehabilitation, and was hooked after a half day in clinic. I matched into a physiatry residency, continued to teach two aerobics classes a week, traveled once or twice a month to my boyfriend's games (during football season), was able to take educational leave back to my health spa in Mexico to learn about acute management of sporting injuries in the recreational population, and was eventually appointed chief resident of my program. At last I decided to apply for a post-residency fellowship in sports medicine. In addition to my transcripts, letters of recommendation, and personal statement, nearly every one of my extracurricular activities added to my resume. My experiences as an avid sports fan, dancer, and fitness instructor with extensive exposure to the issues of elite athletes made me a strong candidate for competitive fellowships. Now I have a career that incorporates my outside interests with my professional duties, and I love it. I truly took advantage of many opportunities to have fun along the way, and all that fun ended up enhancing my career. If you are disciplined enough to make the necessary sacrifices, smart enough to learn the material, wise enough to preserve your sanity, and lucky enough to remain healthy, you will maximize your potential. These tips can help you achieve your goals and gain the competitive edge you need to succeed in medicine and science. Trust me… I'm a doctor.

CHAPTER 10

Meeting Yourself at the Crossroads: A Personal Journey through Medical School

By Marcus Lorenzo Penn, M.D.

Introduction

I have a rather unique yet nontraditional perspective of my experience with medical school. Medicine was not a childhood dream of mine. I did not have parents or grandparents who were physicians. I did not have a long lineage of physicians in the family, nor was I in line to join or take over any private practice from a close relative, friend, or associate. I have received my medical degree, though I am not currently practicing medicine. What I share with you in the following chapter may surprise you, reach you, and hopefully teach you something about the common yet often unspoken reality that goes with the medical school process.

My Background

What led me to medical school was a deep-rooted, fundamental love of science and concern for the welfare of people. What helped me tremendously throughout the process of medical school was having an older brother with whom I shared a desire to be in medicine. He is my only sibling and, at the time, he was already in an M.D./Ph.D. program in San Francisco, California (our hometown). So before I even started medical school, I was privy to unlimited firsthand information regarding the process. My brother had completed his first two years prior to my matriculation. We have always been close, and I have always seen my brother as a mentor. I could always depend on him to give me the honest truth about any situation. Thus, I took his advice regarding my academic betterment as the truth and I followed it.

Let me take a moment to say that my brother was not what you would call an "average" student. He performed at the highest level academically, from grade school to high school and in undergrad. So prior to medical school, I had a very good example to follow academically. In addition, our family always held educational excellence at a premium. I never resented my brother's achievements as we grew up. Quite the opposite occurred, actually. As I watched my brother excel, I felt more motivated to do as well or better than he did. I would say a healthy "motivational competitiveness" developed between us. My brother and I attended the same schools from kindergarten to undergrad. As I spoke to people about my plans to enter medical school, they would say, "Are you following in your brother's footsteps?" I would kindly reply, "Not exactly. I observe my brother's footsteps and then blaze my own trails."

I am not writing this chapter to talk about my brother. What I am trying to do is paint you a picture of my perspective and the circumstances leading up to and following my entrance into medical school. My goal here is to provide information and guidance as a "big brother," if you will, to those of you who truly desire an honest look inside the life of one medical student. I realize that not every medical school applicant has the privilege of an older sibling who has already successfully gone through the application process and completed the first two years of medical school. That is why I feel it is important to share with you the lessons I have learned along my journey through medical school. I hope that you will learn from my mistakes and avoid some of the pitfalls I went through. I believe it is important to hear testimonials about medical school because it allows each person to hear how different circumstances can play into the decisions people make. Utilizing my experiences as examples, you can compare and contrast your approach to entering medical school with that of others, and also find out what methods may be most beneficial for you.

Undergraduate Years

Upon entering undergrad, I sought to model my academic experiences after my brother's experiences. He advised me which classes to take, so I took them. He advised me to perform community service, so I participated in it. He advised me to become my college's Health Careers Society president, so I became it. Soon, I began to feel the pressures to succeed from my brother, my mentors, and myself. I particularly felt the pressure from my brother advising me to capitalize on the mistakes he had made.

In the midst of all my surrounding pressures, I did have an experience that would eventually serve as my ticket into medical school. With German as my minor in college, I went to Frankfurt, Germany, after my freshman year and volunteered at a university hospital. Interestingly, this was my very first exposure to medicine. Naturally, I was quite nervous and self-conscious. I worked alongside nurses, medical students, and other physicians tending to hematology-oncology patients. I was proud of myself for creating this experience, because it allowed me to distinguish my college experience from my brother's.

My Germany experience served as a microcosm of the medical school environment. My four weeks felt more like four years. Each week I had a different challenge to confront. I had to function in a foreign environment; struggle with self-confidence; network with the nurses, medical students, and physicians; interact with patients; and record and interpret medical information in German. This experience was unique, I admit. However, the personal qualities that I used—discipline, perseverance, adaptation, communication, and patience—are common to many people and can be used in various arenas, particularly in medical school. We are all tested at some point in our lives, whether at school, at work, or at home, to pull out parts of our character that we may not have known existed (or that lay dormant). What I wish to impart to you is to take record of those special experiences, and constantly remind yourself of what you can do in tough circumstances. Drawing from these experiences comes in handy with medical school interviews (and in medical school itself), when interviewers give you hypothetical scenarios to manage. In hindsight, I may not have reminded myself as much as I needed to. It could have saved me some heartache down the road.

During my junior year, I went through a serious period of doubt and depression. I was feeling very overwhelmed. I had too much on my plate that year, yet I did not want to let anyone down. I didn't realize I was really only letting myself down. Dealing with tough classes, preparing for the MCAT (Medical College Admissions Test), serving as my college's Health Careers Society president, and participating in extracurricular activities, I felt myself coming to a breaking point. I was seriously considering taking a semester off from school. Looking back now, I learned that you must follow your heart as you enter the medical school process. It's important to be clear that this is *your* dream not someone else's. Any inconsistencies will show themselves eventually if your drive is not genuine.

After some serious soul-searching, I decided against taking a semester off. This decision came only after I dropped some tough classes and took on a lighter load. My personal standard of commitment told me that if I started something, I finished it. I was not going to give up. Soon thereafter, I regained my footing and got back on track. There still followed a long period of recovery and reaffirmation, however. As I went through this period, I realized something about myself and others like me who are largely achievement-driven. Sometimes your drive for achievement may be illogical and you don't know it. You have to be careful when you are achievement-oriented, where you simply achieve for the sake of achievement and not for your own sake. Ultimately, your self-fulfillment will come from the latter, not the former.

During this process, I was still able to study for and take the MCAT, and apply to medical schools, all while I was feeling my academic strength increasing. The MCAT consists of three sections: verbal reasoning, physical sciences, and biological sciences. Fifteen is the maximum number of points you can get in any one section. I used an MCAT prep course that actually increased my overall score by four points. If you have the funds, I would suggest using a prep course, especially if you had used one before and received positive results. When applying to various medical schools, I started with those in my home state. Then I ventured to others I found to be in desirable locations (near family, in a fun city, in a familiar city, or in a city where I had connections). I attended a historically black college in Atlanta, Georgia, and my health careers adviser suggested that I should also apply to historically black medical schools and universities. His advice got me into medical school. Since it has become even more competitive to enter medical school today than at the time I entered, I would advise you to use any advantage you have to get your foot in the door. If you don't, it's not just your loss, but also someone else's gain.

My senior year, I was accepted to a historically black medical school in Washington, D.C., and a grand sense of validation came over me. This was largely in part because it turned out to be the *only* medical school I was accepted to. Ultimately, upon my graduation from undergrad, I felt on top of my game and eternally grateful to my health careers adviser.

Medical School Year One: Can I Do This?
After getting settled in Washington, D.C., I began to feel a sense of fear starting to creep into my spirit. The last day of orientation week, my fellow students and I took a class picture in front of the

medical school. By this time, my fears had come to fruition. I remember wondering, "Why should I take this picture, if I am not sure I will even be here next semester or next year?" There were so many negative thoughts going through my mind at that time that I did not have room for positive ones. This was not the best way to start medical school, though at the time, I was unaware that this is common to many medical students. I asked myself, "Aren't any of the other students scared?" They certainly didn't show it as far as I could see. It would have been so helpful to know I wasn't alone feeling the way I did. I was feeling overwhelmed before I even had my first lecture. One thing I learned, though, was that some classmates hid their fear really well. I wanted to share my fears with other classmates, but my pride kept me from voicing my feelings. If you find yourself in this situation, it's good to talk to someone anyway. Venting your feelings can always help. At some point in our lives, we all have to let go of our pride to get the help we need.

So there I was, in the very first lecture of my medical school education, already scared and insecure. Not quite what I had expected after finishing college "on top of my game." It didn't take long for doubt and depression to come. It was as if they were waiting outside my door and I let them in. I felt them siphoning my spirit to nearly zero. My sanity also seemed to be in a constant tug of war. This led me to go and see the college of medicine's student retention psychologist. She allowed me to voice my struggles and vent my feelings. Still feeling I needed another outlet, I made an appointment with the university psychiatrist. I discussed with her many questions that had plagued me: Why am I here in medical school? Am I here for my family or myself? From where did my original drive for medical school derive? These were tough questions that I knew I could not answer in one session. I had a little snap back to reality when the psychiatrist suggested I take medication to help me feel better. I remember saying to myself, "Damn, I'm not doing *that* bad." I kindly declined the suggestion and did not return after that visit.

Always, in the back of my mind, I worried that I would be forced to buy a one-way ticket back home after flunking out of school. Other times, I just wanted to buy a ticket and quit medical school altogether. This, among other things, I recall discussing with my father one day over the phone. I was telling him how I did not want to continue any longer. I also told him I felt many different emotions welling up inside of me. My father said, "If you feel you need to cry, then cry! Let it out!" So after we got off the phone, I did cry. I remember repeating out loud, "Lord, get this devil out of me!" as the tears fell down my face. Later on, as I became closer to my classmates, I discovered that many of them had broken down and cried at some point during medical school too.

The conversation I had with my father was an important moment for me. It not only served as a red flag to my family that I needed them, but it also served as a release for many pent-up emotions. My pride kept me from asking them to come across the country to see me for a while, but my family, the intuitive family that they are, came to my aid anyway. Each member of my family (Mom, Dad, and brother) came out individually to spend time with me. I needed each of their visits and I told them so. Each contributed something that filled a void I was feeling. I even had an uncle call me from back home in California to encourage me. One of the first things you must do after have starting medical school is get over your ego telling you that you can do it by yourself, because I can honestly say that you can't. I needed my family the whole way through. For some of you it may not be family; it may be a friend, a roommate, a mentor, a pastor, or someone else close to you. The point is to realize you cannot go through this journey alone.

One of the highlights of my first year of medical school was when I went home for Thanksgiving. I went with my family to a cabin in Lake Tahoe, California. Extended family came as well. I remember telling my aunt (my mother's sister) that I didn't really feel like going back to medical school. I remember her saying to me, "Don't worry, sweetie. You'll go back and you'll still finish this year. I believe in you." I felt amazingly comforted after she said this. I realized thereafter that I could hold on to the confidence of my aunt and my family when my own was not enough to support me. I was surprised, yet reassured, by my aunt's matter-of-fact tone when I spoke with her. It was as if she didn't have a doubt in her mind.

Unfortunately, after that wonderfully motivational trip with my family, I returned to my classes still unfocused, lost, and without concentration, but I did continue to go to my classes. My legs took me to my classes, but my heart was not in it. Without consciously thinking about it, I honestly believe it was my aunt's words that kept me moving. Classmates could even see my expressions (or lack thereof) revealing that I was at the crossroads. I remember particular classmates who took me aside to talk with me. I can recall one female student from California who, during lecture, gestured to me that she wanted to talk with me after class. When lecture concluded she asked me, "Are you okay? You don't look so good." I didn't know her too well then, but I sure felt comforted to know that someone was observant enough to see my plight.

A quality friendship developed from that point on. I have many other examples where classmates came to my aid just at the right time. I call them my "medical student angels." Each one helped me go a little further than I thought I could.

While in medical school, it's important to form alliances with other students. I noticed early on that many students who did not do this, or students who spent most of their time alone, did not remain at school. This does not mean you need to be in large study groups to survive; it simply means that it can be very beneficial to find a person or several people with whom you can relay information back and forth. It also helps to know, beforehand, the environment where you learn best. I knew classmates who studied at the library, at school, at home, or even at various Starbucks locations around the city. The key is to discover what works best for you.

Once you have discovered your personal learning techniques, be sure to make use of them and really own them. Discover whether you are a visual learner, a repetitive learner, a learner who listens to lectures, or a learner who studies at home. Ideally, you should have an idea before entering medical school, but for some it may be better to use a trial-and-error approach to finding what best suits you. I, for instance, felt reassured when I was in lectures taking notes, seeing pictures and diagrams, listening to explanations, and asking questions. I discovered early on that I am a visual learner. I also found mnemonics to be extremely useful in my studies. There is so much information given in medical school that it is a must that you find as many associations as you can as quickly as you can.

A major point that my mother had brought to my attention was that much of my difficulty and depression could be attributed to the losses I experienced while in transition from college to medical school. I feel this may be the case for many medical students. Living in a new and unfamiliar city, not having friends (and study partners) from college, not having any relatives nearby, and not having the same level of confidence during college are all voids you may be faced with. The strategic person that she is, my mother, an educator, advised me to write two lists—one column with my losses and another with solutions to those losses. This proved to be very therapeutic for me. It allowed me to put my burdens on paper and off my mind. It is crucial to find coping techniques that enable you to handle the rigors of medical school. We are all unique, so different things give us comfort. The key is to discover and utilize them as early as you can.

After some initial self-resistance, I spent considerable time and effort trying to come up with workable solutions to fill or compensate for my voids. Writing in a journal was one of the solutions I used to relieve my mental burdens. I started to deal with failure as a reality that was a part of medical school—a reality that had been less of an issue for me in undergrad. My perspective on my classes changed from "gotta get an A" to "gotta get a passing grade." I was not lowering my standards. I was simply being practical. I also dealt with not being able to know everything for an exam by knowing as much as I could remember. Even after adopting this new mode of thinking, I still had further growth to achieve.

One day I had a long phone conversation with my mother. Within the conversation she simply asked me, "Can you commit to trying to finish medical school?" and I recall having a really hard time saying yes. After a lot of back and forth, a moment of clarity finally came to me. I told my mother that I was not going to take myself out of medical school. My only way out was if the school dismissed me. Almost instantaneously, I felt a huge mental burden lifted. At that point, the door that had let in doubt and depression was beginning to close. Soon thereafter, I started to feel my spirit rise. I began to see opportunities of community service as a good outlet for me. I particularly sought out those that involved children. Working with children has always been a passion of mine. As I became involved in various children's health initiatives, I felt validated by my gift to connect with children. It put value to the blood, sweat, and tears I had put into medical school thus far. I would advise you to implement some community service in an area of your interest as soon as you feel comfortable with your courses. It can serve as a constant reminder of your purpose for being in medical school.

Despite all my trials and doubts, the one and only class I failed was anatomy. This was the class where I spent most of my time being unfocused, lost, and distracted. I eventually retook anatomy in the summer and passed it. My ego was seriously boosted after completing that class and my first year of medical school successfully.

Medical School Year Two: My Time of Emotional Growth

Returning to school for my second year, I noticed that many classmates did not make it through the first year. I thought that many of these students were doing better than me in school. Looks are very deceiving. What you see on the surface only reveals so much. My brother always advised me not to compare myself with other students in the class. That's an important lesson to learn about medical school: try not to compare yourself to fellow classmates. It can do you more harm than good.

This time I did something different. It was something I had neglected to do in my first year. Before I had my first lecture of the second year, I made a declaration of what I intended to achieve. A week before classes started, I made a promise to myself and to God that I was going to perform my absolute best this year. With that goal set, I knew it would be a much different year than my first. When you make a declaration to yourself or to anyone else, it automatically holds you accountable, and that can be a powerful motivating force to help you succeed.

I started my second year armed with a renewed spirit and an arsenal of rediscovered principles, techniques, and discipline that I had used to succeed in undergrad. Bringing them back into the scope of my daily operations felt amazingly familiar and comforting. I will share them with you with hopes that they will guide you in developing your own tailored game plan.

I started to incorporate more balance into my schedule. I created a morning exercise ritual once I found out how good it made me feel for the whole day. It included using free weights in my room or a quick thirty-minute workout in the apartment gym—just enough to get my blood circulating. This eliminated that groggy feeling in the morning that I had felt during the first lectures of the day. This helped me start each day primed and ready to absorb information. Balance does not have to come from exercise, though it helps; it could be from meditation; taking a walk; getting up early to read new or review old material; or just watching TV. Whatever you do, try to get the end result of feeling relaxed and ready to learn. This will leave you feeling empowered as you take on each new day.

As I began to feel more confident and comfortable with my studies, I would go out on some weeknights. I hadn't done so before because I was afraid my studies would suffer. Sometimes, alone or with friends, I would go to see a movie, have dinner, or go to a poetry reading. This kept me connected to my personal interests and helped diversify my focus. I also felt tremendously proud of myself for being able to do this, and in the process I got to know a few classmates a little better and formed new friendships.

Eventually, I developed a reward-based system that I found to be quite motivational. Whether it was getting Krispy Kreme doughnuts with friends after our exam or going to my favorite chicken wing place, I always had something to look forward to. I also found that having certain rituals helped to balance my stress level. Going alone to the park or somewhere else quiet to meditate, to think, or to not think at all, can also be very beneficial. This proved to be quite successful for me before, during, and after taking an exam. It served as a decompression technique of sorts that allowed me to reset and refresh myself whenever I needed it. At other times, to get myself moving, I did not think of a motivation, but rather a mode of action. I found creating to-do lists very useful, especially when the course load was heavy. Checking off each completed task was quite rewarding.

Another technique I found useful when I studied was starting with uncomplicated courses first and finishing with the more challenging ones. This will help you to get a jump start. Set time limits for each subject, with less time for the easier courses and more time for the challenging ones. This not only gives structure to your studying, it also allows you to cover a lot of information in a limited amount of time. I found this to be the Golden Rule of medical school. By the time you get to the more challenging courses, your mind will be ready to concentrate, and you'll start with a feeling of confidence and completion. Sometimes, listening to music may relax you while you work. I know it worked—and still works—for me.

Like many other medical students, I had good days and bad days, and the bad days were often plagued with feelings of loneliness. I did not have a roommate with whom I could share my feelings. I chose to write my own quotes on personal issues as a means of venting. When I look over them now, I see how my emotional growth is revealed within each quote. This collection of quotes, which I still add to today, will forever serve as a window to my emotional growth.

Previously, I mentioned how important it is to keep balance in a daily routine. With this in mind, I was able to take exams with less fear and feeling more relaxed. Prior to exam periods, some classmates let me know their personal rituals. Some wore the same outfit every time, others stayed up the night before, and some would not stress at all. I was no exception. I would wear something special to my exams. "Look good, feel good, do good," I would say to my friends. These rediscovered principles, techniques, and discipline paid off for me, because my second year was by far the best academic year I had in medical school.

I feel it is important to mention that at this point in my matriculation, my brother decided to take time off between finishing the Ph.D. and returning to complete the last two years of medical school. This was a very difficult decision for him to make. I found out that he had challenges with self-motivation, self-confidence, self-esteem, and "can't do it-ness" and even considered not returning to medical school at all. This was a big shock for me. As I enjoyed the highs of my second year, my brother experienced the very lows of his medical school tenure.

For the first time in my life *I* had to be *his* big brother and offer him words of encouragement and motivation. This was indeed a surreal experience, yet it was a necessary paradox in our lives. It would have been quite difficult for us to have helped each other if we had been at our low points simultaneously. Suffice it to say, it was truly a blessing for both of us. We could not have needed each other more. What I learned from this experience, and I hope you will too, is that the various roles you play in life can change at any moment. The best way to be prepared is to function in a manner that would make you proud to serve as an example for others.

The first board exam you will take in medical school is Step 1 of the United States Medical Licensing Examination (USMLE). The USMLE Step 1 is a grueling eight-hour exam, and you are given seven sets of approximately fifty questions to complete in one-hour segments. This is an exam of knowledge as much as it is of endurance. So when Step 1 came up, I took no chances. I rented a hotel room away from the city and took the exam in a city thirty miles outside of Washington, D.C. I made sure not to have any distractions as I started the exam. I don't suggest everyone go and do what I did before the exam; however, I would advise you to do whatever it takes to get to a point where you feel comfortable that you can function at your most optimum level.

I made two phone calls the night before the exam. The first was to home. I needed to hear the encouragement from my family. My brother's words to me were, "Man, you *know* you have already passed the exam. All you have to do is take it." Those words resonated with me and gave me comfort. The second call was to a fellow female classmate who always had a positive attitude and outlook. I needed to connect with both of these sources before going into the eight-hour exam. I actually had a pretty good amount of sleep the night before, considering what was to come. That morning, I still performed my regular exercise routine. As I sat down before taking the exam, I said to myself, "I have done all that I can. I have no regrets, and I would not do anything differently." Ideally, this is how you want to feel before taking *any* exam. Following those eight long hours, I left the exam standing tall, full of pride for what I had just accomplished.

For the fruits of my labor, I rewarded myself with a trip to Rio de Janeiro, Brazil, with my best friend from college. Many other classmates also took trips after the exam. I can't express to you enough the importance of rewarding yourself after a major or minor victory throughout your medical school experience. If you deny yourself this, you may find it difficult to validate your varied accomplishments.

Medical School Year Three: Listening to Yourself

After my trip, in the days before I started my third year, my father decided to come out and visit me. My USMLE Step 1 results came during his visit. This was a very frightening moment for me, but it was counteracted by my father's presence being there. Before I had the results, I felt as if I had been waiting to exhale. With my father beside me, I opened the envelope. The letter said I had passed! I exhaled, and a wonderful feeling of relief came over me. I found out later that many other classmates did not pass Step 1 of the USMLE on their first try, and they were unable to progress to the third year until they did. What a vivid and constant reminder of how far I had come!

The one thing medical school has truly taught me is that it is as much a mental experience as it is academic. There is discouragement around you everywhere. You will hear about failed exams, dismissed students, and discouraging instructors. The key to your survival is to consciously draw attention away from these negative distracters. I wish I had had that insight before going into my third year.

I completed my first rotation of ob/gyn (obstetrics and gynecology) and went into my surgery rotation. I heard so many horror stories about surgery rotations. In hindsight, I believe I heard one too many of them. I negatively psyched myself out before even starting the rotation. I had done this before—let go of past achievements to hold on to the fear of new ones. I threw away all of my rediscovered principles, techniques, and discipline. "Why do I do this?" I asked myself at the time. Before I could even answer the question, I had failed my surgery rotation and also the next neurology rotation. Then I really got scared about failing medical school. Once again, I had opened the doors of doubt and depression.

I knew I felt burnt out mentally, physically, emotionally, and academically. I seriously considered taking time off from medical school. I knew that I needed to take a step back from all that was going on. I was headed in a direction that I did not like at all. It was difficult to decide how much time off I needed. One month, six months, or a year were thoughts bouncing around in my head during that time.

At a point when I felt the most invalidated, I experienced something that did quite the opposite for me. I attended my school's annual alumni scholarship ceremony and was surprised to be the recipient of the Most Improved by the Third Year award.

It was extremely validating to be recognized by my medical school for my accomplishments, especially at a time when I was having difficulty recognizing them myself. What came from this was my choice to finally take full ownership of where I was at the time and to act accordingly.

It was during my following rotation, internal medicine, that I finally decided to take a personal leave of absence. I remember my mother said to me then, "To rest on the road does not end the journey." Her wisdom confirmed my decision. I later spoke with the academic dean and discussed a plan that would work for me. My ultimate decision was to take a leave of absence for the remainder of my internal medicine rotation and make up the rest of the time when I returned. This still allowed me to graduate on time with my classmates, and it was very important to me. I spoke with other classmates and medical residents and, surprisingly, many regretted not taking time off during or after medical school. Medical students and residents alike rarely discuss this thought.

I went back home for forty days. Within that time, I was able to reflect, reaffirm, and recharge myself. I knew I needed to be with my family, and it sure felt good to be in their presence again. While home, I promised myself I would start back renewed. I returned and finished my third year, passing all of my remaining rotations with a newfound resilience, confidence, and comfort that I had not felt before. I believe your ego can sometimes lead you into thinking that any sign of weakness is a bad thing. I am here to tell you that by acknowledging your weaknesses and giving yourself the time you need to heal (whether forty days or just forty minutes), you can make a huge difference in your performance.

Medical School Year Four: Understanding Who I Am

Going into my fourth year of medical school, I knew how to pass exams and rotations. I had been through hell and back. However, I will admit there was still a hint of fear inside of me before each exam, though fear never overcame me. I would not let that happen again, even if fear was present. I remembered writing the quote, "Fear never holds on to you. Only *you* can hold onto fear." So I began to let go of the fears that plagued me. The small fears that did remain, I believe, kept me grounded and taught me not to take my progress for granted. I now knew what worked for me, and I also knew what to keep in balance for optimum results. You should always have this balance as you go through medical school. I stayed connected to the community by working at many health fairs. This helped me remain focused as I completed medical school. I remember how good it felt to contribute to the health of my community. I also realized how much I enjoyed being an authority figure and having knowledge to share for the benefit of others.

Four months before graduation, a family emergency completely caught me off guard. My mother suffered a seizure, and this would eventually lead to the diagnosis of a brain tumor. I flew home that day to hear the details of her diagnosis and to tend to her. I had to make a difficult decision to return to school after going through this ordeal, but I did return after spending a week at home. I knew I had to finish medical school.

Two months after my mother's initial seizure, I flew home for the scheduled surgery to remove her tumor. The date of her surgery happened to be two days before I was scheduled to take Step 2 of the USMLE, the last board exam before finishing medical school. I came to the realization that you can't control what circumstances arise in your life. You can only control the responses to them. I knew I could not let these circumstances stop me from succeeding in my task. Before I took the exam, I reassured my mother that she shouldn't feel guilty about her condition. I waited through another long period of anxiety and then got my exam results. I had passed with the minimum score. Considering all that I had gone through, I was not surprised. I was thankful just to pass.

As the last months of school drew to a close, I saw my classmates' joy when they researched possible medical residency programs. I could not share the same feelings, because one thought would not pass from my mind. The vision of my next year was not clear. I was also feeling some residual burnout. Then it dawned on me that many classmates had had careers or jobs before entering medical school, and others had taken time off before starting. They were able to see what life was like in the "real world" outside of medicine and outside of school. I did not have this perspective, having come directly from college to medical school. This realization made me feel better. I took a long time to come to the realization that taking time off before, during, or after medical school was not a taboo. I learned earlier in medical school that when you need to take time for yourself, you should take it. I started to see myself as an investment, and time invested in me would facilitate many positive results. Our lives are just too precious not to take the time to reexamine our goals. I recall the words of author, philanthropist, and professor Cornell West: "An unexamined life is not worth living."

I also seriously thought about what I really wanted to do. Perhaps I had jumped the gun on a medical career. Maybe there was something else I needed to experience before going back into the medical game.

Old questions resurfaced in my mind: Was I in medical school for me or for someone else? Where did my desire to be in medical school originate? Was I following my dream or a learned template? Perhaps I had allowed the "motivational competitiveness" between my brother and me to get the upper hand. I did not ask myself, "Do I want this for *me*?" when I needed to. Perhaps my focus had been only to achieve and not necessarily to achieve in what I was interested in. I felt the need to address these questions and issues before leaping into a medical residency program.

Graduation came right on time, and my family was there to root for me as I walked across the stage to receive my medical degree. What a glorious day it was! At times I had thought I would never make it to that stage, but I did, and I thank God for it. At my graduation party, my brother acknowledged how hard it must have been for me to be the younger brother of such an accomplished older brother. His statement also made me acknowledge and understand the pressures I had put upon myself to achieve like him. A week after my graduation, I flew to San Francisco to see my brother receive his medical degree. It was during this ceremony we both acknowledged how we had pulled together to help one another get through the arduous process of medical school.

In the months after graduation, I sent an e-mail to my undergrad German professor. I described to her how I had lost my direction within the process of medical school. She quickly retorted that I must have still had *some* direction, since I had received my medical degree! It didn't occur to me until then how right she was.

Reflections Following Medical School

I have realized that surviving medical school is more about defining personal levels of excellence and discipline in conjunction with having the support of family and friends than it is about comparing accomplishments with others or trying to outperform those around you. While combating feelings of mental doubt, wanting to drop out of medical school, and wondering if medicine is the life for you, the aforementioned factors can prevail and help you rise above your circumstances. The human will is a powerful thing and can amaze you. Looking back at my experiences, I realized that I hadn't given myself enough credit for all I had accomplished. Medicine is a very long journey, which makes it too easy to lose track of how far you have come. At some point between college, medical school, and medical residency you have to stop, look back, and see what milestones you have achieved. This is the best way to validate your ongoing progress. This is where I am now in my journey, and I believe the time I take now to reflect on my progress so far will prove golden in the years to come.

I believe life has by nature—and by God's design—a cyclic balance to it. I believe every experience in life has an equal and opposite experience to complement it. Thus, we can always learn a lesson from our own life experiences and those of others. This is what I hope I have provided for you in this chapter—a compilation of lessons I've learned that can benefit you not only in medical school but also in life. As we go through life, let's take advantage of the lessons life teaches and use them as our own competitive edge. Then we can perpetually go onward, moving others and ourselves to a higher state of awareness and wisdom. Regardless of whether medicine is the life for you, always strive to follow your heart and find your passion. If you find that it does lie in medicine, all the better—it is then that your true life's journey begins.

Questions to ask yourself before medical school:

Are you comfortable with being an authority figure in society?

How do you handle death and suffering?

If a career in medicine doesn't work as expected, do you have a plan B, C or D? What other careers that use your science background do you find interesting?

Does your interest in medicine lay in patient care or the science behind medicine?

Do you want to work with patients (or a particular type of patient) or are you interested in analyzing medical results and assisting with patient care?

Will you feel guilt if you choose not to enter a career in medicine?

Do you have a strong will to complete tasks and hold yourself accountable for the results?

Are you a person who can sustain delayed gratification for an extended period of time?

Do you feel you need a career in medicine to validate yourself or can you find self-validation outside of a medical career? How do you personally find self-validation?

Do you handle adversity head on or do you shy away from it? How well do you recover from setbacks?

Can your interest in medicine sustain you through long and sometimes unrewarding days in the hospital, clinic, and/or medical office?

Section Three

Resisting Conformity:
Charting Your
Own Course

CHAPTER 11

Leveraging Your Strengths

By Suzy Jones

As director of business development for a major biotechnology company, I feel extremely fortunate to have a job that I enjoy so much. I am consistently challenged and continuously learning and leveraging my strengths. I believe I am making a contribution to society—helping to bring novel drugs to market that address significant unmet medical needs. As I reflect on my career thus far, I never thought in a million years that I would be working in business development, or for a biotechnology company for that matter. Early on in my academic career, I set out to become a physician. Even though I ended up taking a left turn that led me down a path other than traditional medicine, I have had a very successful and fulfilling career to date. I attribute my success less to my technical expertise or things that I learned in textbooks than to my ability to leverage lessons learned from my diverse life experiences—which has inspired me to tackle new challenges, leading to an evolving self-awareness. In this chapter, I share my personal experiences with the reader to demonstrate how creating a "mental toolbox" of lessons learned from one's own experiences can help ensure successful outcomes when encountering obstacles or new situations. By mental toolbox, I mean a collection of distinct memories from those life experiences that were pivotal in evolving your awareness of self—things you learned about yourself when you overcame a major obstacle, when you accomplished something that nobody thought you could, when you exceeded your own expectations, and especially when you failed miserably. To create a mental toolbox, you need to find the value in what you perceive to be both positive and negative life experiences so that you can leverage the lessons you learned from these experiences at a later time. One thing to be aware of is that sometimes the most valuable experiences in your mental toolbox can come from the most unlikely places, so don't discount any experience that may help to shape who you are.

My biotech career spans fourteen years, and includes experience working in discovery research, trying to develop new drug candidates; in product development, managing multiple drugs at different stages of their product lifecycles; and in business development, identifying and negotiating new licensing opportunities. In the absence of a postgraduate degree, I have been successful at navigating my way through different career opportunities—climbing the job ladder in each role. I attribute this success to the solid science foundation I obtained from my undergraduate education and the experience I gained on the job, combined with some very strong assets in my mental toolbox: confidence, determination, people skills, and integrity. Since most of the readers of this book are on their way to developing a solid science foundation, I will focus the rest of this chapter on personal life experiences that gave rise to the assets in my mental toolbox and tell you why these particular attributes are important to anyone who plans to hold a senior-level position someday.

Confidence

My peers often tell me that I exude confidence. It is true that I always believe I will have a successful outcome when I take on a new project. This confidence came from a culmination of life experiences, where I learned that I could excel in any environment, under any circumstance. Growing up in a very supportive, low-income, African-American community while attending some of San Francisco's most prestigious non-integrated private schools was probably my earliest and most influential experience that taught me who I was and what I was made of. Several things that would follow this defining experience would reinforce my belief that I could excel at anything I chose to pursue.

I grew up in a single-parent home with my mother and two older sisters. In an effort to escape the violence and limited educational choices of West Philadelphia, my mother, a playwright, moved her three daughters across the country to San Francisco when I was just five years old. On an artist's salary, my mother raised us in the Western Addition, a predominantly African-American, working-class neighborhood of San Francisco. Like many mothers raising children in low-income neighborhoods, my mother would stress the importance of education to us every day and did everything in her control to give us a chance to fulfill our dreams. She would escort the three of us to the city bus every morning, past the neighborhood characters who hung out on our stairs all night, to San Francisco's most exclusive private schools. Somehow, she managed to get us scholarships to these schools. We would take several buses in our secondhand clothes while the other kids in the latest fashions were being dropped off in fancy cars by their family drivers. It was an interesting dichotomous experience—living in such a lively, low-income neighborhood yet spending my weekdays in a world of privilege.

I was very much an integral part of both worlds. In school, I was more athletic than most of the boys, consistently got the lead in the annual school play, was the editor of the school newspaper, and was competitive academically. I was also very involved with organized sports in my community. In these environments, I was able to develop a sense of belonging—an awareness of how similar I was to my academic peers, despite our cultural and economic differences, and an awareness of how similar I was to the people in my neighborhood, despite my elite educational opportunities—all of which led to a competitive spirit with an appropriate sense of humility. In retrospect, I could not have written a better script to prepare me for my career in science; my ability to thrive in both environments gave me the confidence to perform and be myself in any situation. Although I did not know it at the time, this confidence was the first attribute I added to my mental toolbox, and it has proven to be the most valuable one throughout my career.

Confidence helped me manage my scientific failures and develop a healthy attitude about being challenged on a regular basis—a common experience in science. The seven years I worked in exploratory research was, hands down, one of the most challenging experiences of my life. I was one of only two African-Americans in a research function of three hundred people, where the mode of operation was sink or swim. Data was openly challenged in department meetings, which is where experimental failures were openly disclosed. While most people were happy to share their knowledge with you, there was no one at the company who had the job of mentoring me or ensuring my success. I had overcome some big challenges in my life up to this point, but I had always had a support network of family, tutors, and mentors. My confidence in my ability to learn and work through tough problems enabled me to deal with humbling experiences in this new phase of my life, even in the absence of a support network. It gave me the courage to show up to work with my tail wagging the next day, even if I had gone home the night before with my tail between my legs. This was how you swam in this environment—there was too much to learn and no time for low self-esteem or self-pity. My strong belief that I could overcome adversity from my past experiences enabled me to conquer my challenges in research and ultimately to contribute to several novel discoveries. In addition, I coauthored several papers, which were published in accredited scientific journals alongside some of the world's most accomplished scientists. Even more valuable than my scientific achievements, surviving research gave me more confidence than ever that I could do anything I wanted to do with my science career.

Determination

Scientific training teaches you to validate theories and hypotheses by trying to poke holes in them or prove that they are incorrect. In my opinion, this rigorous training has also had an impact on how people with strong scientific training react to novel ideas that don't follow a conventional dogma. Whether one is proposing a new approach for tackling a problem or pursuing a career path that is unconventional, these ideas are almost always met with skepticism. Sometimes the most novel discoveries, or best outcomes, result from unconventional approaches or out-of-the-box thinking. People with a strong sense of determination are more likely to pursue novel approaches or pathways in the face of skepticism. These approaches are usually associated with increased risk, resulting in high rewards when the outcome is positive.

It was during a high school experience that was eye-opening that I developed a sense of determination that would later prove to have a profound affect on who I was to become as a person. Shortly after graduating from middle school, I learned that I would not be attending high school with my fellow classmates. Even after being offered a partial scholarship, my mother could not afford to send me to private school anymore. Instead, I attended an inner-city public high school along with all the kids from my neighborhood. It was at the public high school that the plight of so many of the kids from the neighborhood became painfully apparent to me. The classes available to us—particularly the kind that developed analytical thinking skills—were limited; there were never enough textbooks, and on several occasions not even enough chairs in the class for all of the students. Worst of all, the teachers and counselors had low or no expectations of the students beyond graduation, particularly in math and science. I felt sorry for my peers, who, unlike me, did not have a superior primary school education and, in some cases, did not have a supportive environment to go home to at night. Having these advantages enabled me to transcend the lack of inspiration on behalf of the public school administration and not let it defeat my spirits. On the contrary, public high school motivated me more than ever to pursue my dreams, and solidified my commitment to helping others.

By this time in life, I had decided that I wanted to become a doctor, and I was determined to not let anything get in my way. I had something to prove to all of those counselors who had written certain students off as blue-collar workers and to the students who were to come after me—they needed to see people like them, from their neighborhood, from their school, achieve goals. This experience had such a profound affect on me that to this day, almost every time anyone tells me I can't do something, I do it—and usually better than it has ever been done before. When confronted with new challenges, I know I can always draw on my determination and will to succeed. I have yet to be confronted with a problem or challenge in the corporate environment that compares in magnitude with some of the challenges I had to overcome in public high school.

Having a strong sense of determination will give you the drive to find solutions to complex problems that present themselves on the job. When I moved from discovery research to product development, I was responsible for managing teams accountable for moving products through their product life cycles. As the person with limited project management experience, I was given a product that was thought to have minimal risk associated with it; it had just been approved by the federal Food and Drug Administration and was thought to have limited commercial potential. The product was part of a very dysfunctional four-party partnership, with two of the partners located in other countries. I was determined to make this global partnership the most highly functioning partnership in the company. I utilized team-building methods to help build trust between all the parties and to improve communication. Several team members were skeptical about whether these methods would result in an improved relationship, but after some coaching, I was able to get them to participate anyway. They did, in fact, become the most highly functioning team in the company, working together to resolve issues and find the best path forward for the product. After I had successfully managed the partnership for three years, the product became the top revenue driver for the company and one of the biggest oncology products in history. The experience also proved to be one of the best learning experiences one could ask for in this industry: I learned about drug development and how to commercialize a drug, and I gained a lot of experience in managing partnerships. It also reaffirmed my belief that sometimes the biggest opportunities are those where the most problems exist. Once again, my mental toolbox came through for me. I was determined to succeed in this role, and I did.

Many students reading this chapter will be able to identify with my experience in public high school and will have a deep sense of determination to achieve their goals as a result of people they encountered along their journey who told them that they would not succeed. One caution I would give these students is this: be careful to not let your determination to succeed adversely impact your decision-making while you are in pursuit of your goals. I was determined to become a physician because I had a strong will to help other people, I loved science, and I wanted to be respected. I exploited every opportunity to increase my chances to get into medical school: I completed a premed major, I attended summer research programs, and I volunteered in hospital settings. When I was finally confronted with the decision to go to medical school in my second year of employment as a research associate in biotechnology, I did not go. Instead, I opted to roll the dice with the field I was already in.

This was one of the most difficult decisions I had ever made. I felt sad to let go of a dream I had clung to all of my life, and even worse, I felt a deep sense of failure for not having completed something I had set out to do—I did not want to let my family and friends down. While the decision was difficult, it was the right one and ultimately came down to lifestyle and business considerations. For the first time in my life, I was questioning my desire to want to be around sick people all of the time. I also had a difficult time thinking about incurring so much debt over a period of time when I would not even be contributing to my 401(k) plan. Lastly, I was excited about the new path that I was pursuing in biotechnology—the work I was doing was fun, challenging, and still enabled me to fulfill my desire to have an impact on patients' lives.

This experience reaffirmed my ability to take risks and taught me that my identity was not attached to being a physician. There were several ways I could fulfill my science objectives and leverage my strengths without becoming an M.D. This detachment of my job from my identity enabled me to once again evolve my awareness of self. From this point on, I wanted to make career decisions based on my excitement level about the learning opportunity. In retrospect, I realize that like so many other students studying science, my desire to become a physician was based on my own—as well as society's—limited exposure to all the things I could with a science education. There is a very positive social prestige attached to being a physician that is not accorded to someone who develops drugs. Before my biotechnology experience, I equated being a physician with being successful, but after being exposed to the opportunities in biotechnology, I began to equate success with my ability to align my career objectives with experiences that were meaningful to me. I wanted to take on roles that were exciting to me while leveraging my strengths to make a significant contribution.

People Skills

Not all senior managers or leaders have good people skills. I have a personal bias that the best leaders are those who have great people skills, and therefore, I have chosen to talk about them here. By people skills, I mean an ability to communicate, work well, and build relationships with people from various backgrounds or cultures, including people who have perspectives that are different from your own. Some people say that people skills are innate— either you have them or you don't. I don't subscribe to this theory. I also don't believe that you can learn these skills from reading a textbook or taking a class. Developing good people skills comes from having diverse experiences—experiences that enable you to function outside of your normal environment by dispelling stereotypes that you had assumed to be true and teaching you to appreciate the differences and find the similarities between you and others around you. My ability to embrace a wide range of opinions, perspectives, and communication styles has proven to be critically important in helping me to work effectively in teams, to lead teams, to collaborate with partners from all over the world, and, most importantly, to influence outcomes. Being able to influence a group of dissimilar people with varying perspectives to arrive at a consensus is a necessary skill for any leader today, where work is accomplished in teams and through global partnerships.

I had so many diverse experiences growing up in San Francisco, a tolerant city for all kinds of lifestyles and a melting pot for many different cultures. The predominantly African-American neighborhood in which I grew up bordered on the fringes of Japantown. The close interaction with our Japanese neighbors prompted my mother to send me to a Japanese after-school program to learn the language and the culture. I was the only non-Japanese child in the group. Learning a new language in an environment where I was the only one who did not know the language was eye-opening and challenging. Initially, I was not treated very well and got into several fights with kids who teased me. I eventually found some common ground with my classmates, though, and made some friends that I still have to this day.

This experience gave me a heightened sensitivity to others who found themselves in a similar predicament, such as the Vietnamese and Cambodian students who had recently migrated to San Francisco with their families and had to attend my high school. Their names were butchered by the teachers on a daily basis, and they were treated unkindly by all the other students for being poor and clueless about American culture. My high school was made up of African-American students from the Western Addition, middle-class Chinese students from the Sunset district, low-income Chinese students from Chinatown, Latino students from the Mission district, Vietnamese and Cambodian students from the Tenderloin neighborhood, and just a few Caucasian students from the Fisherman's Wharf neighborhood where the school was located—talk about a melting pot! I was one of the few students who managed to break down the racial barriers at my school to build relationships with students from all backgrounds. I played on the basketball team with my African-American peers; I played on the softball team, which was predominantly Chinese; and I was the president of the Spanish language club. These experiences, along with the overall experience of growing up in San Francisco, impressed upon me an appreciation for people who are in some ways different from me, and an awareness of how similar we all are, even if we come from very different places. These insights have motivated me to stick up for the underdog, to bridge gaps between people who don't initially understand each other, and to find the common ground when people disagree. Collectively, these experiences have helped me to find solutions when others can't see a clear path forward.

This unique perspective on diversity was very helpful to me during my time as a project manager, when I managed multiple collaborations and considered myself to be the resident expert on making them work. I was responsible for ensuring that we worked well not only as a team within the company, but also as a global team along with our European and Japanese partners.

In the transition to my business development role, where I am responsible for leading a team of people to identify and negotiate new license opportunities, my people skills have been instrumental in making me a great negotiator, a respected member of the business development team, and an effective manager of people. I have developed excellent communication skills and a special ability to build trust with people in just a short time period. In negotiations, these skills are helpful in understanding the needs of the other party, resulting in the ability to get deals done quickly. As a manager, I have leveraged these skills to better understand the needs of people who report to me, enabling me to develop their talents and inspire them to excel in their careers.

Integrity

Building credibility is essential to having a successful career in a corporate environment. Credibility comes from acting with integrity, even if it means that you have to openly disclose when you do not know something or when you have made a mistake. In order for you to become an executive within a company, the CEO needs to know that he or she can trust you to be honest and to act with integrity—not to be right all of the time. This is an attribute of all of the executive members of my company, and I admire them for it. They have set a moral standard for the rest of the company, and nothing short of this standard is tolerated.

Sometimes it can be difficult to openly disclose when you have made a mistake, especially when that mistake may result in a loss of money to the company or a major time delay on an important project. One thing to remember is that you are part of a team whose members are all working toward a common goal. Nothing that happens at the company is about you or your needs, but rather about the needs of your customers—in the case of biotechnology, the patients who will ultimately receive the drug products. Openly disclosing mistakes in a timely manner will result in the opportunity to resolve the problem most efficiently; it may also provide both you and the company with a valuable lesson that may prevent this mistake from ever happening again. While it can take some time to build credibility by acting with integrity, it only takes one incident of acting without integrity to lose your credibility, resulting in the potential loss of your job or possibly even a poor reputation that could hurt your chances of being hired by other companies or institutions. As a child, I never got in trouble for openly discussing the mistakes that I made; only the ones I tried to hide. I also learned early on that by disclosing and dissecting my mistakes, I could improve and evolve as a person. As an adult, I made a vow to myself that I would not compromise my integrity for any job. And I feel fortunate to work for a company that would never put me in the position to ever have to do so.

Conclusion

Even though I did not pursue my original plan to become a physician, I have had a very fulfilling and exciting career. My business development job has been the most fun and exciting position I have had to date. I travel all over the world looking for novel opportunities, I negotiate and structure deals that directly contribute to the success of the company, and, most importantly, I have an opportunity to influence decisions that could have an impact on the lives of patients. I'm not sure what my next career opportunity will be, but I know it will be exciting, it will be challenging, and it will draw upon all of the diverse experiences I have stored away in my mental toolbox to date to be able to make much bigger contributions.

In this chapter, I focused on how my mental toolbox attributed to my success by helping me overcome challenges in the corporate environment. I believe that many lessons you will learn on your life journey can be leveraged to overcome challenges in any environment. Consider the following things as you plan your next career move: (1) Read the chapter entitled, "Expanding Your Horizons: Alternate Careers in Science." The information will educate you on additional career options available with a science background and provide you with information to prepare yourself academically for the career that excites you the most. (2) Keep an open mind to new opportunities that present themselves to you—even if they were not a part of your original plan. (3) Revisit and dissect your pivotal life experiences, and see how you managed to deal with them. This process will help you to heighten self-awareness and grow. (4) Develop and draw from attributes in your mental toolbox, because these experiences will help you to conquer challenges that you may encounter in your lifetime.

CHAPTER 12

Expanding Your Horizons: Alternate Careers in Science

By Suzy Jones

Introduction

Many people who have an affinity for careers in the sciences want to be able to look back on their lives at some point and know that they made a significant contribution to society or had a positive affect on the lives of others. This chapter will focus on nontraditional career paths that could provide opportunities to fulfill this quest. Being well informed about different career options is helpful in preparing for a career. Therefore, the objective of this chapter is to expose you to a variety of careers that are not commonly discussed or well documented. This will allow you to make more informed decisions about how to invest your time and money from this point forward to achieve your goals.

In addition to increasing your awareness about a myriad of career opportunities, you can increase your chances of having a fulfilling career by gaining an awareness of the kind of experiences you want to have in life and by being open to new opportunities that may provide you with these experiences. The following questions are a good place to begin the process. Do you like working with people? Do you like working with sick people? Do you like working under intense pressure? Do you like being challenged? Are you a leader or a follower? Are you an individual contributor or do you prefer working in a team? What are your values? Having a good sense of your values will influence your decision-making process along your journey and will have a significant impact on your career and overall job satisfaction. So as you review the different jobs described below, I want you to keep a couple of things in mind. First, with every job or position, the details vary from company to company; the descriptions below are based on my personal knowledge and experiences. Second, view the information as a starting point—make sure you actively build on your knowledge base by doing additional research on opportunities that may be appealing to you. And finally, take a deep breath and relax—you are ahead of the curve. You can take advantage of your solid science foundation to explore several different career paths. If you believe in yourself, it is never too late to change your mind and decide you want to pursue another option.

Discovery-Focused Jobs

Research Scientist

Individuals who gravitate toward careers in research usually have a natural affinity for science and discovery and are driven by their desire to uncover the underlying mechanisms that elucidate the reasons why things are the way they are. Research scientists enjoy troubleshooting difficult problems and like being consistently challenged. They perceive challenges as opportunities, which is important, because these individuals experience more failures than successes during the course of their research careers. Job satisfaction comes from having the opportunity to make novel discoveries, publishing these discoveries in peer-reviewed journals, and being respected by their peers. For these reasons, next to the discovery itself, publication is the ultimate experience for research scientists, because it validates the novelty of the discovery and provides a platform of communication. It gives them an opportunity not only to share the information for the furtherance of science, but also to showcase their work for review by their peers. The more distinguished the journal, the bigger the accolades.

A day in the life of a research scientist will vary dramatically, depending on whether that person is working for an academic institution or a company (biotechnology, pharmaceutical, technology platform, or medical device).

Academic Scientist

Research scientists in academic institutions will have more opportunities to collaborate or interact with others in their respective fields. They also have the freedom to determine which scientific questions their lab will address. This freedom does not come without a price—depending on the size of the lab, most academic research scientists are required to write grants to gain funding for their programs. Their ability to obtain grant money will also dictate the job security of some of the researchers, which could create a lot of stress. The viability of their labs is also dependent on their ability to identify important, unanswered questions and then demonstrate that they have also identified a feasible approach to addressing these questions. For some, academic research is not considered a job, but rather a life's work—it can sometimes define who they are. Because of this, research scientists tend to work long hours alongside their postdoctorate students and research associates. Individuals who want the freedom to dictate the direction of the work being conducted in their lab and the opportunity to teach while conducting their own research and who enjoy close interaction with others in their respective fields should consider pursuing a research science career in an academic environment.

Industry Scientist

Research scientists in a company setting are motivated by the potential to discover novel products, either drugs or devices, that will improve the lives of patients suffering from diseases. They enjoy some of the inherent luxuries that come from working in a corporate environment, such as access to abundant resources. Yet they retain some of the culture of an academic environment; many biotech or pharmaceutical companies feel like an academic environment and sometimes refer to their work site as a campus. The academic feeling comes from a mixture of the start-up company atmosphere that most biotechnology companies adopted from their high-technology neighbors, combined with the academic culture that most scientists brought with them when they left their academic posts for industry positions. For example, there is intense pressure to publish in an industry environment; some biotechnology companies have a publication and citation record that is on a par with some of the most prestigious academic institutions. While research scientists in a company setting do not have to write grants, they are accountable to senior management to help meet the company's goals. This means that job security in this role comes from the ability to discover novel drug candidates or devices consistent with the company's corporate objectives. This also means that the company can decide to kill the project that a scientist has been working on and assign that scientist to another problem—sometimes in a completely different therapeutic area.

Individuals preparing for career as a research scientist should consider an undergraduate degree in the physical or natural sciences and should exploit opportunities to conduct research during that time. This may give them insight into the scientific discipline that most interests them and help them identify a Ph.D. program at an academic institution that has a solid reputation in that specific discipline. After completing a Ph.D. program, students should pursue a postdoctoral fellowship in a reputable lab, preferably in an academic setting. For those students considering a research career in industry, the postdoctoral emphasis should be in a disease-focused area—do not study yeast or *Drosophila* (fruit flies). While most biotechnology and pharmaceutical companies have well-established postdoctoral programs, these companies tend to have a narrow, well-defined focus for discovery. A program in an academic setting will provide the postdoctoral fellow with access to a broader range of intellectual thinkers, which will be more conducive for ensuring adequate mentorship and guidance to help hone the future scientist's bench skills and intellectual thinking abilities. Outstanding training and publication history can make a fellow more marketable upon completing the postdoctoral program.

Development-Focused Jobs

Toxicologist/Pharmacologist

Individuals who have a desire to apply their science education toward developing drug candidates as opposed to discovering drug candidates should consider careers as toxicologists or pharmacologists. These scientists are responsible for translating drug candidates that come out of research into safe therapeutics. They do so by conducting preclinical programs to evaluate the appropriate dose, regimen, and overall safety profile of a product prior to having that product tested in humans. Specifically, they evaluate the pharmacokinetics (rates) and pharmacodynamics (action) of the products to determine the maximum safe dose, and provide insight into the design of the Phase I studies. Most toxicologists/pharmacologists can expect to work more predictable hours than discovery research scientists. While toxicologists/pharmacologists work under tight timeline pressures, their careers are dependent on their ability to successfully carry out the experiments required to evaluate the lead drug candidates—unlike the research scientist who has the added pressure of coming up with novel discoveries to help the company maintain adequate growth over time.

Individuals considering careers as toxicologists/pharmacologists should consider graduate programs in veterinary medicine or Ph.D. programs in biology, biochemistry, pharmacology, pharmacokenetics, or pharmaceutical sciences. Students who pursue Ph.D. programs in biology, biochemistry, or pharmacology should consider doing a postdoctoral program, which would not be necessary for students who get an advanced degree in pharmacokinetics/pharmacodynamics or toxicology. There are currently not enough toxicologists or pharmacologists to fulfill the current demand in the United States for these positions.

Manufacturing/Process Science Scientist

Individuals who are more process- and detail-oriented, like working in a more structured environment, enjoy working in teams, and don't want to work with animals should consider opportunities in manufacturing or process sciences—the two major functions in most companies that are responsible for drug supply. The company must be able to provide sufficient worldwide quantities of drugs to patients who need them.

The major role of a scientist who works in process science for a company developing biologics is to identify a stable cell line that can produce sufficient quantities of a lead drug candidate and to develop a process to scale up quantities so that sufficient amounts are produced to meet the needs of the clinical study and eventually the market. This includes developing the process for production, purification, and recovery of the product, ensuring that the overall yield for the process is cost-effective. This usually involves a continuous effort to develop cutting-edge process development processes and methods of purification to improve the overall cost of goods for the product. These scientists also work very closely with the marketing and clinical teams to determine and develop the best formulation of the product to address the unmet needs of the patients.

A manufacturing scientist is responsible for executing the process development plan flawlessly, so that every vial of product is identical. This includes implementing the process of manufacturing the product, testing the product for impurities, putting the product into vials, and shipping the product to distributors. The manufacturing scientist is also involved in long-term planning for the company, helping to determine the size of the manufacturing plant needed to support the growth of the company.

The lifestyle of scientists working in process science and manufacturing can be very stressful. The ultimate goal is to ensure that no patient who wants a drug product ever has to go without it. One small glitch in a very complicated process could jeopardize an entire lot of material. This mistake could cost the company but more importantly, it could impact the lives of patients. Additional pressures can come from tight timelines for plant capacity and unanticipated market demands for the product. A close relationship with the marketing team is essential in order to be able to forecast drug demands and guarantee up-to-date forecasts on market performance.

Students considering a career in process science or manufacturing should consider pursuing a bioengineering degree from undergraduate institutions with manufacturing sciences programs. Because many of the large companies have training programs for their specific processes and systems, a postgraduate degree is not required to obtain an entry-level position in these fields. However, a Ph.D. in molecular biology, chemical engineering, analytical chemistry, or synthetic chemistry (for individuals interested in companies who focus on small molecule drug development) would provide the broad knowledge base to support a long-term career. Ph.D. candidates should consider postdoctoral programs in a corporate environment to get the appropriate experience that will make them competitive for scientist-level positions in process sciences or manufacturing. Given the growth of the biotechnology and pharmaceutical industry, individuals with expertise in process and manufacturing sciences are in demand and are well compensated, especially at the scientist level.

Clinical Scientist

Individuals who have a desire to have a broader influence on medicine than one patient at a time should consider working as clinical scientists in the biotechnology or pharmaceutical industry. These clinical scientists design and conduct large, definitive, clinical trials to determine if a new drug candidate will have a positive benefit for patients with a particular disease. A unique difference between this experience and that of an academic physician is that academic physicians typically participate in small, exploratory clinical trials and rarely get to see the overall clinical trial data until it is published; they also continue to treat patients while conducting their clinical research.

The job responsibilities for a clinical scientist in a company setting include designing clinical trials for new drug candidates, protecting the integrity of the clinical trials, determining whether the data from the studies is believable and interpretable, and, most importantly, ensuring the safety of the patients participating in the study, both during and after treatment. The clinical scientist works closely with researchers in the company, to understand the mechanism of action of the drugs; with the manufacturing team, to ensure that the company can make enough of the drug to supply patients; with the regulatory team, to facilitate close interaction between the company and the Food and Drug Administration (FDA); with the marketing team, to understand the broader marketplace for the product; and with community physicians and academic centers, who will participate in enrolling patients in the trial.

Clinical scientists in general tend to be very committed to their profession and, as a consequence, usually work long hours in a very stressful work environment. The stress is associated with the corporate pressure to meet study timelines, as well as the pressure associated with awaiting the outcome of the studies. The studies are usually very large and very expensive, with costs in the tens to hundreds of millions of dollars. Additionally, the patients are sometimes extremely sick, and their participation in the study usually represents a last chance at life. But while the stress level is high, the overall job satisfaction for clinical scientists is also high— they have an opportunity to create paradigm shifts in the treatment of patients suffering from terrible diseases. It is not uncommon for a clinical scientist to receive personal letters from physicians who have exhausted treatment options for their patients and are given hope with an additional treatment option, as well as from patients who have benefited from treatment and have been afforded more time and/or a better quality of life. These experiences can help to keep clinical scientists both grounded and focused on the most important aspect of their jobs—the patients.

Students interesting in becoming clinical scientists should complete a medical degree and a residency program. Students who want to pursue a career as a clinical scientist in a company setting should have at least two years of clinical experience after their residency program before applying for a corporate position. While some companies do not require an employee to have an M.D. to work as a clinical scientist, this is not the norm.

Regulatory Manager

Individuals who have excellent organizational skills, pay close attention to detail, like interpreting regulations, enjoy negotiating and troubleshooting, and can be extremely diplomatic should consider a job working in a regulatory group for a company. Regulatory managers are responsible for managing the interactions between the company and the FDA. They can specialize in one of three areas: the regulation of the manufacturing and preclinical program, the regulation of the clinical program, or the regulation of the advertising and promotional program. Regulatory managers coordinate documentation that outlines how the drug will be manufactured and tested, and, most importantly, they help to ensure that the company is in compliance with FDA regulations. A job is this area can involve educating the company on FDA regulations, educating the FDA on the science supporting novel drug candidates, and negotiating with both entities to gain alignment on an approvable development plan and on the final language that will appear in the package insert for the product. Individuals working in this environment can manage a good work/life balance, with the exception of the period of time in which a project is in the middle of a major regulatory filing.

Most issues that arise in this role are scientific in nature, so a solid science education and an understanding of statistics and clinical data are essential. Strong communication and management skills are also important. The minimum requirement for a person interested in this type of job is an undergraduate science degree, and work experience in a regulatory environment is highly desirable. For example, experience working in the manufacturing, quality, or clinical department of a biotechnology or pharmaceutical company could suffice. Individuals without an advanced science degree would be eligible for an entry-level position in a regulatory group. In general, a person who aspires to become the director or vice president of a regulatory affairs department should possess a Ph.D. or M.D. degree with several years of regulatory experience. Regulatory managers with several years' experience are well compensated and are highly sought after both for their expertise and their established rapport with the FDA. As the United States and European regulatory authorities continue to work together to align the regulations in both territories, the job market for these individuals is expanding.

Business-Focused Jobs

Lawyer

Students who enjoy both science and law should consider a career as a lawyer for a biotechnology or pharmaceutical company or with a law firm that works with these companies. There are a myriad of jobs for lawyers in a company or firm setting. The most common ones include: a litigation lawyer who is responsible for representing the company in legal matters when a suit has been filed on behalf of or against the company; a corporate business development lawyer who is responsible for negotiating and drafting contracts for new collaborations; a patent lawyer who is responsible for determining the corporate patent strategy and managing the company's patent portfolio; a commercial lawyer who is responsible for working with the internal marketing team and the FDA to ensure that the company is in compliance with all rules and regulations; a clinical lawyer who negotiates and drafts contracts with outside clinical research organizations and study sites for outsourced services; and an employment lawyer who is responsible for ensuring that the company is operating in compliance with employment regulations. All of these positions require excellent written and oral communication skills, solid negotiation skills, and a comprehensive understanding of corporate, patent, or employment law.

The big difference between working with a law firm representing science-based companies and working for the company itself is the lifestyle and the breadth of experiences on a daily basis. Lawyers associated with a firm tend to work longer hours and are generally better compensated than lawyers employed by a company, if you don't take stock options into consideration. This is because they are compensated based on the number of hours they can bill to the company/client for services rendered—the more they work, the better they are compensated. Their jobs can be challenging because they often lack the historical context from which the project was derived and they do not have the autonomy to make decisions on behalf of the company. Lawyers working within a company generally work a normal nine-to-five day. They have the added benefit of witnessing the impact of their efforts on the company, whether it is defining a new long-term collaboration, securing an important piece of intellectual property, helping to get a clinical trial enrolled, keeping the company from violating the legal guidelines for promoting products, or defending the company in a big lawsuit.

Individuals pursuing careers as lawyers should have a strong science background and a law degree. While it is not necessary to have an advanced science degree for all of the jobs that lawyers can perform in this setting, it is highly recommended. To be sure that they have the appropriate training and are competitive for a legal position in the corporate setting, students should strongly consider pursuing a Ph.D. in a broadly applicable discipline like molecular biology or biochemistry (particularly for patent law), a law degree, and at least two years' experience in a firm setting.

Sales Representative

Individuals, who possess a natural selling ability, have an entrepreneurial spirit, are self-motivated, and want to work flexible hours outside of an office or lab setting should consider working in sales for a biotechnology or pharmaceutical company. Sales representatives are assigned a territory for a given product and are responsible for selling that product directly to physicians in their territory. They run their territories like their own business. Their success is largely dependent on the quality of the data demonstrating that their product will benefit patients, their ability to understand and communicate that data, and their relationships with the physicians in their territories–which, if they are good, help them to get more of the physician's time during office visits. Sales representatives who are successful are generally well compensated. A typical pay structure for a sales rep includes a base salary plus commission based on sales performance relative to established goals.

The experience necessary to be hired as a sales representative varies, depending on the product being sold. If the product is targeted to a primary care market and is sold to general practitioners, an undergraduate degree in science is sufficient to compete for these opportunities. Most large pharmaceutical companies like Merck and Co, Johnson and Johnson, and GlaxoSmithKline routinely hire students right out of undergraduate science programs. By contrast, if a product is targeted to a specialty market and is sold to physicians in fields like oncology, neurology, or dermatology, the sell is more data driven and requires a more in-depth understanding of science. Many companies that hire for these positions look for individuals who have prior experience in a hospital setting, either as a registered nurse or as a sales representative, with at least two years of primary care experience. An advanced science degree like an M.S., Ph.D., or M.B.A. is a plus for these specialty markets but is not mandatory.

Marketing Manager (Product Manager)

Individuals who enjoy strategic planning, are business-minded, and have strong analytical skills should consider marketing as their career. Marketing managers have the responsibility of managing the life cycle of a given product; therefore, they are also referred to as product managers. They are ultimately responsible for managing revenues and expenses for a given product through the creation and implementation of a comprehensive marketing strategy. Product managers need to have excellent analytical sense and ability, well-developed project management skills, an ability to digest clinical data, and good oral and written communication skills—they interface with people in other functional departments on a daily basis. For example: with clinicians early in the process, to define the unmet medical need or market opportunity; with the process science team, to provide input on the formulation of the product; with the regulatory managers, to produce promotional materials and to negotiate the language in the final package insert with the FDA; with the field sales force, to train them on how to position the product in the marketplace; and with key opinion leaders, to speak to them about their experiences with the product. To be successful in this role, product managers need to have a strategic focus and need to be able to use their analytical skills to determine what is driving the business, how to differentiate their product, and what levers they can pull in the market to move the business forward. Their role is highly visible in most organizations and could lead to great leadership opportunities.

To pursue a career in marketing, students should pursue a science undergraduate degree and an M.B.A. and should consider two to three years of field sales experience. Although not required, an advanced degree in a science discipline is a plus.

Business Development

Individuals who have an interest in both science and business, are very analytical, have strong negotiation and communication skills, are comfortable engaging in difficult conversations, are individual contributors, and are self-motivated should consider working in business development in industry or in a technical licensing group at an academic institution.

A business development job in industry involves using one's scientific knowledge to identify new opportunities (molecules, compounds, technology platforms) that may enhance or balance out the company's pipeline, and then using one's business skills to negotiate the terms under which the company may obtain the new opportunity. If the company is small, the majority of business transactions involve outlicensing the company's core technology to other companies. To be successful in this role, business development managers must be competent at financial analysis, have a solid science background (research or clinical), have some understanding of drug development, be skilled at communicating novel scientific approaches to a broad audience, and possess excellent influence management skills to facilitate decisions within the company to either move forward or kill an opportunity.

A business development role in the technical licensing group of an academic institution involves utilizing your scientific and business knowledge to outlicense the university's discoveries and intellectual property. To be successful in this role, the technical licensing person should have skills similar to the business development manager, but should also be knowledgeable in the area of intellectual property since the majority of the business transactions include providing licenses from the university's patent portfolio to other institutions and to companies.

There are not many business development jobs available within most organizations; thus, they tend to be highly competitive. The business transactions that are negotiated usually result in adding significant short- and long-term value to the organization, which means that business development jobs are also high profile; this translates to people who hold business development jobs, reporting directly to the senior management of an organization. As such, the risks and rewards associated with it are also high.

Students interested in pursuing a career in business development should plan to become experts in science and/or business. While it is not necessary to have expertise in both areas to gain an entry-level business development position in most companies, the ideal candidate has a Ph.D. in an appropriate scientific discipline (a therapeutic or disease focus, immunology, biochemistry, or molecular biology), as well as an M.B.A., and has some real work experience in a functional or operational role (research, development, marketing, or sales).

Venture Capitalist

An alternative to business development for individuals interested in pursuing a career that would allow them to integrate their interest in science and business is working in venture capital (VC). VC firms invest money in start-up companies with the goal of making a good return on their investment. The responsibilities of individuals who work in these firms vary, depending on the specific job titles. Individuals who join a VC firm right out of a Ph.D. or M.B.A. program can expect to enter the firm at an entry-level position as an analyst or associate. The role of the analyst or associate includes identifying and evaluating new technologies to determine if they have scientific merit and downstream commercial utility. A person in this position is also responsible for determining how much money the new entity will need to evolve the technology to prove that it works. Specifically, the analyst and associates conduct the scientific due diligence and financial analysis necessary to enable the senior members of the firm to make investments in new technologies with the goal of growing the fund of the firm. Due diligence requires cultivating relationships throughout the industry to help validate the technology. Because of this, individuals who want to be successful in this role need to possess excellent communication and people skills in addition to their technical capabilities. Analyst/associates are typically paid a very attractive base salary, and they get an annual bonus.

Individuals with five to twenty years of industry experience are eligible to join a VC firm as a principal or partner. These individuals are responsible for fundraising, leading financial deals to help get the new company off the ground, identifying CEOs to lead the new company, and sitting on the board of the new company to give them strategic guidance. They are typically paid a substantial base salary and an annual bonus. Partners also receive a carry, which is a percentage of the firm's profits.

The compensation structure, in addition to the opportunity to be on the forefront of cutting-edge science, makes these jobs very attractive. They are also hard to find and are, therefore, very competitive. Individuals pursuing analyst/associate level positions should have an advanced science degree, an M.B.A. and/or some operational level experience from industry to compete for these positions. Individuals attracted to the principal or partner roles in a VC firms will need substantial industry experience before going to the firm. It is very unusual to move up the career ladder in the firm from an analyst or associate role to a partner role. Scientific, business development, and commercial expertise are all industry assets that would be valued by a VC firm. Last but not least, be aware that VC firms are not seeing the returns that made these jobs so popular during the peak of the dot-com era. If you are considering a career in VC, it is important to understand the risks associated with the opportunity by getting a good sense of the size and performance of the fund as well as the performance of the companies that are being funded.

CHAPTER 13

Discovering Your True Purpose

By Frederick L. Moore, Ph.D., and Michael L. Penn Jr., M.D., Ph.D.

It was during a brainstorming session to uncover a title for this book that we discussed the idea of each person possessing an internal monitor and/or a global positioning system that is designed to help find his or her North. It is in reference to the North Star, that symbolic star that has been used to help people find their bearings for thousands of years. It is our belief that just as each person has a unique path in life; it is through listening and understanding our internal North Star that we are able to align ourselves with our purpose. So, as we talk about the concept of an internal North Star, we will define what this place means to us. We also acknowledge, however, that each of you reading this will have your own definition for this place, and we challenge you to use our concept of North as a reference in assisting you to discover what this indescribable place means to you.

Each person possesses a unique set of talents, gifts, and blessings, and we believe that part of our mission in life is to understand, develop, and utilize these attributes to accomplish our life's goals.

Yet this concept seems to be difficult, because with each decision that we make, there are internal and external forces that can inhibit us from finding our true North. For instance, let's think about how we make decisions in life. Do you make decisions coming from a place of fear? Do you factor in the expectations of your parents, friends, and family members before you make a life decision? Do you believe that there is nothing in life that you cannot achieve if you set your mind to it? Do you view yourself with positive self-esteem? With each decision we make, we need to understand the roots behind those decisions.

Most people place substantial weight on major life decisions such as what college they should attend, what their college major should be, whether they should go to a graduate or professional school, or what kind of job they want when they finish school. And that's all well and good. But remember that the small decisions you make previous to a major life decision have a significant effect on your attitude and environment surrounding your next major decision. For example, let's imagine we are someone, corresponding to the figure on the next page, who is trying to find his or her North. There are positive and negative, as well as internal and external, factors that contribute to each decision we make. And since there is no one "right" path that is required for us to achieve our life's goals, it is the positive factors represented in the figure that help us frame a positive perspective on every experience we have and allow us to find and stay on our right path. If we take a closer look at the type of questions we ask ourselves after a negative interaction, we can consciously learn more about our perspective and begin the process of challenging it. For instance, what were the lessons that you were supposed to have learned from that experience? Did you learn something new about yourself? Can you honestly say that you gave a 110 percent effort when you pursued that endeavor? Why or why not? Could the outcome have been different if you had given your maximum effort? Cultivating and implementing these positive factors as we navigate life can help us to continually grow, but more importantly, it can help us find our North.

+ (positive factors)	- (negative factors)
understanding your strengths	comparing yourself to others
understanding your innate learning style	self-doubt
self-competitiveness	imbalance
self-awarness	negative stereotypes
confidence	living for others expectations
faith	herd mentality
balance	bad habits
	stress
	lack of self-awareness
	making decisions from a place of fear

Definition of North

So what is our definition of North? We first would say that North is a state of mind. When you find your North, you have developed a state within yourself that is at peace; a place where you have unconditional tranquility in response to the actions, challenges, or obstacles that life presents to you. Our second description of North is an understanding of self. When you find your North, you have a deep understanding of your strengths and weaknesses; you also have a deep understanding of the type of experiences and outcomes you want from life, and you are utilizing your talents to make a difference that only you are equipped to make. Michael Crichton is one example of someone who has found his North. After graduating from Harvard Medical School, he embarked on a journey to become a writer and filmmaker, where he utilized all of his talents, including his science background, to become the father of the techno-thriller. He is the only person ever to have had the number-one book, television show, and movie in the United States all at the same time. In addition to his best-selling novels, his accomplishments include developing the television show *ER* and the movies *Jurassic Park* and *Twister*. It is obvious now that Michael Crichton made the right decision to follow his North, but he had no guarantees when he began his journey. And neither do you. Ask yourself, "What would I do tomorrow if I knew that I couldn't fail?"

Interestingly, without realizing it, many people have incorporated some of the negative factors from the previous figure into their decision-making process at some time. Consequently, they live their lives from an out-of-balance state of fear that leads to a path away from their North. For example, when people possess the herd mentality, they don't have the strength and courage to separate from the crowd. Based on a false sense of security, these people tend to never push the limits of their potential; thus, they never discover all of their strengths, and they let the people around them set their goals, determine their level of self-esteem, and influence their view of the world. We challenge you to analyze the negative factors presented in our model and ask yourself, "Are any of these negative factors inhibiting me from finding my North?"

Strategies for Finding Your North

Over the course of this book, different authors have given advice, strategies, and approaches that can be used to help you find your North. Kyra Bobinet details an approach to developing self-awareness and maintaining balance in her chapter, "Striving for Balance while in School." She developed a systematic approach for taking inventory of ourselves, creating pictures of our balanced and imbalanced states, and devising a unique plan to implement, achieve, and maintain a dynamic state of balance. We also discussed how you can develop a better understanding of your innate learning style in the chapter "Reaching Academic Excellence by Discovering Your Innate Learning Style." It is through the process of understanding how our minds work that we edge closer to a true understanding of self. Suzy Jones gives excellent examples of how to develop a "mental toolbox" through understanding your strengths in her chapter "Leveraging Your Strengths." She relates how she developed confidence through her life experiences and thereafter, utilizing this sense of self as a way to identify her perfect career path. Other authors in this book have given examples of decisions they have made based on the expectations of those around them, and how they were eventually able to discern their true feelings. Chad Womack gives a powerful account of his pursuit of medical school for the wrong reasons, and how that process has helped him to find his North. Our goal in presenting to you the diverse examples of each of these authors was to add additional illustrations and perspectives to your growing mental toolbox.

Since it is impossible to describe every approach and technique that people can use to find their unique path in life, we will focus this last discussion on one's attitude during rough times. It is inevitable that people will make bad decisions in their lifetime; it is how we respond to these negative situations that helps us to find our North. Our approach is to adopt the fighter mentality rather than the victim mentality during these times. There will always be a new challenge or adversity to overcome. This is partially because we have no control over our environments, but also because we grow spiritually through overcoming obstacles. So it is our choice to admit that we play a part in every event that happens to us and to acknowledge that there are things that we can learn from each circumstance that we experience. When we play the victim, we take away our responsibility in that situation; we say to ourselves, "This happened to me, and I must experience the consequences," but we are not proactive about changing the situation. In addition, we lose the lesson that we were supposed to have learned. So in essence, choosing the victim mentality moves us away from our North, because the decisions we are making are coming from a place of nonacceptance or denial. Moreover, these decisions are centered on fear. Thus, existing in this state of mind will cripple you and prevent you from being able to reverse situations from a negative to a positive by a change in attitude and creative thinking. A powerful way to find your North is to not react to life as a passive victim, but to act on life as a fighter.

Follow Your North

After you have found your North, you will be constantly challenged to stay on that path. This will require making good decisions about your next steps in life. Since the expectations of others can sometimes pull us from our heart's desire, we must also look for guidance from mentors, peers, friends, and family members who have experience in areas that we are pursuing. We must create and implement a decision-making system that helps us to balance external inputs with our own desires. A crucial part of this system is the ability for us to understand ourselves. This process requires some time and energy. Because we have so many thoughts and ideas running through our minds each day, we need a way to flush them out and analyze them. One approach is to write your thoughts down. We have both discovered that when we spend quiet time in a peaceful place surrounded by our thoughts, it can be a powerful way to uncover our true desires. Some people write down all of their daily activities in a journal. That is a great way to remember what has gone on in your life, but we want to go deeper into the psyche. The goal is to write in a manner that doesn't force your mind to move in any particular direction, yet allows you to express all of the thoughts that come to mind. This exercise allows your spirit to lead you in a direction that it deems necessary for awareness; moreover, it allows you to capture all of your fleeting thoughts, so you can consciously analyze what is really on your mind. Fortunately, this process can be accomplished in many ways, including writing in a journal, typing on a computer, or tape-recording your thoughts.

The next step in your evolving decision-making system is to take in advice from external sources. This is what we call "data collection mode." In this mode you must find a way to listen and store information, yet not be biased by who is giving it. We suggest talking to people with a wide variety of perspectives in order to be able to weigh the pros and cons of all of the advice. The last part of your decision-making system is to monitor yourself to see how the combination of your thoughts and this outside information sits with you. This requires asking yourself those hard questions that will get at the root of your desire to pursue this new life endeavor. Is my decision to pursue this direction coming from a place of fear? Do I have enough information to make a good decision? Do I trust what my spirit is saying to me? If I don't agree with what my spirit is saying to me, what are those reasons? Am I fighting this decision because I don't want to accept the consequences? The more honest you are with yourself during this process, the more you will get from it.

Conclusion

As we move through life, we must understand that it is a process, not a destination or goal that we must accomplish. One of the greatest rewards in reaching a goal is seeing significant manifestations of growth and change at its completion. While they are in school, some students think that they will begin living life after they graduate. They are currently living life. Obtaining a professional or graduate degree in the sciences is a challenging task. The process can push you past all of your perceived limits and then some, but we believe there are approaches presented in this book that you can utilize to help with your journey, and alternate careers that you can pursue when your academic journey is done. The sky is truly the limit, and we hope that we can play a part in helping you find your North.

Kyra Bobinet, M.D.

Kyra J. Bobinet is the executive director and cofounder of Vision Youthz, a San Francisco-based organization dedicated to holistic personal transformation for youth through building diverse service communities and fostering healthy connections to inner self, society, and nature. Vision Youthz serves at-risk and incarcerated youth fourteen to twenty-one years old. Dr. Bobinet is a 1998 graduate of the University of California, San Francisco School of Medicine, and a recipient of the 1997 James Comer Fellowship (American Academy of Child and Adolescent Psychiatry), the 1998 UCSF Martin Luther King Jr. Award, and the 1998 Echoing Green Graduate Fellowship in social entrepreneurship. Dr. Bobinet is of Ojibway, Lakota, and Czech descent, and a mother of two. She has dedicated her life to serving others and affirming the unconditional worth of all beings.

Herbert Boyer, Ph.D.

Herbert W. Boyer has served as a director of Genentech, Inc. since he cofounded the company in 1976 with Robert A. Swanson, a venture capitalist. He also was a vice president of the company from 1976 to 1990. A biochemist and genetic engineer, Dr. Boyer has demonstrated the usefulness of recombinant DNA technology to economically produce medicines, which laid the groundwork for Genentech's development.

Dr. Boyer also was a professor at the University of California, San Francisco, and an investigator for the Howard Hughes Medical Institute. At the time Genentech was formed, he was a professor of biochemistry and biophysics at UCSF as well as the director of the graduate program in genetics.

In 1993, Dr. Boyer was awarded Switzerland's prestigious Helmut Horten Research Award along with Dr. Stanley Cohen of Stanford University for their pioneering research in the use of gene technology in medicine. In 1985, he was elected to the National Inventors Hall of Fame and is an elected member of the National Academy of Sciences.

Dr. Boyer received the Golden Plate Award from the American Academy of Achievement in 1981 and the Albert Lasker Basic Medical Research Award in 1980. He is a fellow in the American Academy of Arts & Sciences and received the Industrial Research Institute Achievement Award in 1982. He is on several editorial boards of scientific publications and has written or co-written more than a hundred scientific articles.

Dr. Boyer received his bachelor's degree in biology and chemistry in 1958 from St. Vincent College in Pennsylvania. He received his master's and doctorate degrees in 1960 and 1963 respectively from the University of Pittsburgh.

Tanya Henneman, Ph.D.

Tanya Henneman, a proud native of Berkeley, California, has demonstrated throughout the course of her life a commitment to community service and academic excellence. Currently, she is the co-chair and creator of the Infinite Possibilities Conference, a conference designed to support and empower underrepresented minority women in the mathematical sciences. She is also committed to the reduction of health disparities and is involved in designing a plan to reduce the rates of hypertension in the African-American community in South and West Berkeley. Dr. Henneman received her doctorate training in the field of biostatistics at the University of California, Berkeley. Prior to attending UC Berkeley, Dr. Henneman obtained a B.S. degree in mathematics from Spelman College and a master's degree in science and engineering from the Department of Mathematical Sciences at Johns Hopkins University. Her academic accolades include a prestigious National Science Foundation Fellowship and a Ford Foundation Fellowship. Outside of academics, Dr.

Henneman has a passion for helping students expand their minds. During her tenure in graduate school, she created and directed a program that provided tutorial services to students of all ages. In addition to teaching students, Dr. Henneman has served as a panelist to many community and academic organizations that aim to disseminate information to underserved communities. These organizations include the Black AIDS Institute, the National Brothers of the Academy Think Tank Conference, and the Minority Training Program in Cancer Control Research. Dr. Henneman has dedicated her life to helping others reach their highest potential.

Freeman Hrabrowski III, Ph.D.

Freeman A. Hrabowski III has served as president of the University of Maryland, Baltimore County since May 1992. His research and publications focus on science and math education, with special emphasis on minority participation and performance.

Born in 1950 in Birmingham, Alabama, Dr. Hrabowski graduated at age nineteen from Hampton Institute with highest honors in mathematics. At the University of Illinois at Urbana-Champaign, he received his M.A. (in mathematics) one year later and his Ph.D. (in higher education administration/ statistics) at age twenty-four.

He serves as a consultant to the National Science Foundation, the National Institutes of Health, and universities and school systems nationally. He also sits on several corporate and civic boards. Recent awards and honors include election to the American Academy of Arts & Sciences and the American Philosophical Society; receiving the prestigious McGraw Prize in Education and the U.S. Presidential Award for Excellence in Science, Mathematics, and Engineering Mentoring; and being named Marylander of the Year by the editors of the *Baltimore Sun*. He also holds honorary degrees from the University of Illinois at Urbana-Champaign, Gallaudet University, the Medical University of South Carolina, and Binghamton University, among others.

He is coauthor of two books published by Oxford University Press: *Beating the Odds* (1998), focusing on parenting and high-achieving African-American males in science, and *Overcoming the Odds* (2002), about successful African-American females in science.

A child leader in the civil rights movement, Dr. Hrabowski was prominently featured in Spike Lee's 1997 documentary, *Four Little Girls*, which chronicled the racially motivated bombing in 1963 of Birmingham's Sixteenth Street Baptist Church.

Suzy Jones

Suzy Jones grew up in San Francisco's Western Addition neighborhood with her mother, and two older sisters. She always envisioned a career in science from as early as she can remember. While medical school was the focus of her academic vision, she realized after one year at Genentech that she could make significant contributions by better utilizing her love of science, business acumen, and people skills in a different role than that of a physician.

As director of business development at Genentech, she is the head of the immunology and hematology group, where she manages a team of dealmakers responsible for identifying new collaboration opportunities that will support the company's short- and long-term strategic objectives. Jones has fourteen years of biotech experience. She spent seven years doing basic immunology research; three years doing product development, where she managed novel cancer therapeutics; and four years in business development executing multimillion-dollar business transactions.

Alissa Myrick, Ph.D.

Alissa Myrick is a postdoctoral scholar in the Division of Infectious Diseases at the University of California, San Francisco. Working at the interface of public health and molecular biology, she is utilizing molecular and field-based approaches to study the mechanisms of drug resistance in malaria.

Dr. Myrick obtained her Ph.D. in biological sciences in public health from the Harvard School of Public Health in the summer of 2003. The major component of her thesis project was the characterization of the *Plasmodium falciparum* multidrug resistance gene at the transcriptional level. During her dissertation, she was given the opportunity to conduct molecular biology training and field research in Dakar, Senegal. She was elected to serve on the Harvard Graduate Council as well as the Student Coordinating Committee at the School of Public Health. She also served as co-chair of the Minority Biomedical Scientists of Harvard and was actively involved in efforts to increase diversity in the sciences.

Dr. Myrick obtained her bachelor's degree in molecular and cell biology from UC Berkeley in 1996. Her experience at Berkeley was enriched by her membership in the Biology Scholars Program, where she became a member of the Student Advisory Committee. Her work with BSP laid a foundation for her commitment to the idea of excellence through diversity. She was an HIV/AIDS peer educator and received a grant to study HIV in Lusaka, Zambia. This experience led to Myrick's interest in interdisciplinary research combining public health and molecular biology.

Frederick L. Moore, Ph.D.

Frederick L. Moore, a native of Fairfield, California, is an optimistic survivor by nature. After experiencing frustration with his elementary and high school education, he began his pursuit of academic excellence at Solano Community College. Thereafter, Dr. Moore attended the University of California, Berkeley, and obtained his B.A. degree in genetics with honors in 1996, and graduated from the University of California, San Francisco, with a Ph.D. in the field of human reproductive genetics in 2002. Dr. Moore is very passionate about assisting people with reaching their highest potential, both mentally and spiritually. In 2001, Moore cofounded the nonprofit organization Brothers Building Diversity in the Sciences (BBDS) with his colleague Dr. Michael Penn Jr. The organization aims to utilize science as a platform to empower underrepresented minority students to pursue careers available with a science background. Dr. Moore has received many academic accolades, including fellowships from the National Science Foundation and the Ford Foundation, but he is most proud of the Martin Luther King Jr. award, received for his humanitarian and community service work from UC San Francisco. Dr. Moore is grateful for his blessings, and is committed to expanding outreach to people who are disadvantaged and/or want to achieve at their highest level.

Marcus Lorenzo Penn, M.D.

A published researcher, recognized scholar, and youth protégé, Marcus Lorenzo Penn is an advocate for culturally competent health-care and administration. Dr. Penn serves as a specialist in this capacity for ethnic and immigrant populations. He is also a community health consultant associated with Health Pact, Inc., whose purpose is to build healthier communities through communication and coordination with health-care service providers and consumers.

Dr. Penn has worked and promoted his strategies for improved health-care quality for the disadvantaged throughout the eastern and northwestern United States, in Rio de Janeiro, Brazil, and in Frankfurt, Germany. He has also worked in the northeastern and southeastern United States, creating and implementing science and health education programs targeting underrepresented minority children.

Dr. Penn is native to and currently resides in San Francisco, California. He received his medical degree in 2003 from Howard University College of Medicine in Washington D.C, and received his bachelor of science degree in biology in 1999 from Morehouse College in Atlanta, Georgia. He is fluent in German and has a working knowledge of Portuguese.

In 1997, Dr. Penn served as Health Careers Society president for Morehouse College, promoting awareness for minorities in health care. His academic honors and awards include the 100 Black Men of the Bay Area Scholar of the Year Award, the Ronald McDonald House Charities/ UNCF Health and Medical Scholar Award, Phi Beta Kappa, Minority Access to Research Careers (MARC) Scholar, and the Sinkler Miller Medical Association Scholarship.

Dr. Penn attributes much of his successes to his late mother, Margaret L. Penn, Ed.D., and his father, Michael L. Penn Sr., M.P.A., for instilling within him the values of faith, family, perseverance, education, culture, and community. In his leisure time, Dr. Penn is a writer, photographer, and world traveler. He identifies himself as spiritually grounded and experientially connected to all those around him.

Michael L. Penn Jr., M.D., Ph.D.

Michael L. Penn Jr. is committed to diversifying the landscape of science and medicine. Born and raised in San Francisco, Dr. Penn attended Morehouse College in Atlanta, and then went on to complete a combined M.D./Ph.D. program at the University of California, San Francisco, in May 2003. Spending time with students is his passion. Dr. Penn has devoted countless hours advising hundreds of students during his career. In 2001, he cofounded a nonprofit organization, Brothers Building Diversity in the Sciences (BBDS), with his UCSF colleague Dr. Frederick Moore. The mission of BBDS is to utilize science as a platform to empower underrepresented minority students. Dr. Penn is also dedicated to preserving and promoting public health, having served as a health commissioner in San Francisco from 2002 to 2004. Currently, he is a product manager in BioOncology marketing at Genentech. He feels grateful for the ability to impact his community positively through his employment at Genentech, Inc., his former tenure on the San Francisco Health Commission, and community service through BBDS.

Brandee L. Waite, M.D.

Brandee Waite is a California native, born and raised in the San Francisco Bay Area. She attended Stanford University, where she received a bachelor's degree with honors in human biology. She attended medical school at the University of California, San Francisco, and completed her residency in physical medicine and rehabilitation at Stanford University Medical Center. Following residency, she joined the faculty at Johns Hopkins Medical Institute for a fellowship in sports medicine. She is a contributing author on several musculoskeletal/ sports medicine research projects and texts. Aside from pursuing her medical career, Dr. Waite also spent a year teaching fitness classes at a resort in Mexico and on an international cruise ship. She is an avid dancer and continues to teach weekly kickboxing and step aerobics classes in addition to working full time as a physician. The second of five children, Dr. Waite enjoys spending time with her family, watching football, and traveling. She loves Mexican food, a good laugh, and scary movies. She attributes her success to the grace of God, a supportive network of friends and family, and her predisposition to approach every task with enthusiasm and optimism.

Malik White, M.D.

Malik White spent his formative years in a small city in Northern California. After attending San Jose State University and earning a B.S. degree in the biological sciences, he went to New York City to matriculate at Cornell University Medical College, from which he received his M.D. degree. He then returned to the Northern California area to complete internship and residency training in general pediatrics at the University of California, San Francisco.

For the past six years, Dr. White worked as a general pediatrician in several large hospitals in the San Francisco Bay Area, New York City, and Los Angeles. He cared for patients from numerous ethnic backgrounds and all rungs of the socioeconomic ladder. His work focused on treating patients in the neonatal intensive care unit, the general pediatric hospital setting, and the pediatric trauma emergency room.

Desiring to work with extremely sick children, Dr. White is currently enrolled in a training program at the University of California, Los Angeles, to specialize in pediatric critical care medicine. He plans to eventually join the faculty at a major medical school, teaching medical students and providing care for children in the intensive care unit.

Chad Womack, Ph.D.

Dr. Chad Womack is the chief executive officer and chief scientific officer of NanoVec, a privately held biotechnology company that is developing novel gene delivery vectors for the next generation of vaccines and immunotherapeutics. Most recently, Dr. Womack was a senior research fellow at the NIH Vaccine Research Center (VRC), where he was the head of the HIV section of a viral pathogenesis laboratory. At the VRC, Dr. Womack's research concerned the immunopathogenesis of HIV/AIDS in developing countries and HIV/AIDS vaccine development. Dr. Womack was the first Ph.D. graduate student to matriculate at the Morehouse School of Medicine, where he earned his doctorate in 1998. His dissertation research was titled "Molecular Epidemiology of HIV/AIDS in Rural Georgia." He received his B.S. degree at Morehouse College in 1988, graduating cum laude in biology. Dr. Womack's research program has involved both domestic and international research collaborations with scientists in India and Africa (Nigeria, Botswana, and South Africa).

Outside of his research activities, Dr. Womack is cofounder of the National Association for Blacks in BIO (NABB), and serves as a member of the International Scientific Advisory Board for the Gede Foundation/ Gede AIDS and Infectious Diseases Research Institute; the board of directors of the Women's Collective, a nonprofit organization dedicated to addressing the specific needs and improving the lives of HIV-infected women in the Washington, D.C. metropolitan area; and the board of directors of the Black AIDS Institute, a nonprofit organization that serves as an African-American think tank on HIV/AIDS. In addition, Dr. Womack is a past president of the NIH Black Scientists Association (BSA), and a member of the Office of AIDS Research Planning Group for Racial and Ethnic Minorities; and a member of the joint NCRR/NIAID/ OAR working group for RCMI faculty working on HIV/AIDS and health disparities at Historically Black Colleges and Universities (HBCUs).

Visit us at

FindingYourNorth.com

Providing a sustainable environment that allows individuals to translate knowledge & experience into a fulfilling science-related career.